In the Days
of Our
Resilience

December 2020

–

May 2021

Ellis —
hope it's okay
that I profaned
your name in
this modest
book of poems.

NATHAN BROWN

Karen insisted...
-L-)

(see page 280)

Nathan Brown

...

MEZCALITA
PRESS

MEZCALITA
PRESS

Mezcalita Press, LLC
Norman, Oklahoma

In the Days of Our Resilience

December 2020

—

May 2021

NATHAN BROWN

Table of Contents

January ... ...

Introduction

In the Days of Our Resilience: December 2020 – May 2021, Book 4 of the Pandemic Poems Project, represents the culmination of one of the darkest, strangest, most life-altering, and yet still wonderful in a few weird ways, years of my life and professional career, not to mention our species as a whole.

These commissioned poems tell the stories of contributors from around the globe, and they track the slow crawl toward some sort of beginning of the end of a brief and bizarre epoch, a great pause in human business-as-usual.

Few things have affected more how I perceive myself as an artist, as well as what the artist's purpose is in the scope of history. I've been humbled and inspired at the same time. And I have discovered that audience is more than *appreciation*… it is *participation* in art.

Video readings of these poems can be viewed in the Fire Pit Sessions on my Facebook page:

https://www.facebook.com/chinacoman

Acknowledgements

Book 4 is dedicated to Konrad and Darra Eek. It's been one hell of a year… and, as of now, we are still here. Feet on ground. Cocktails in hand. Eyes forward. And to Brian Franklin. Hang in there brother. Somehow. Someday.

Also to my wife, Ashley, and our friends, Liz McIlravy and Sarah Flournoy, the Muses who inspired the Pandemic Poems Project.

Mom, Dad, Sierra… always and forever.

Many thanks to Milton Brasher-Cunningham, the Music Director of the Fire Pit Sessions, for so much help and support over this year.

A special thanks to all who have hosted me in your homes, taken care of me, in my travels over the years. You make what I do possible.

And finally, thanks to those who contributed, topically and financially, to this project. Your generosity rescued me from a fiscal washout. My gratitude springs eternal.

~ Nathan

In the Days of Our Resilience

MEZCALITA
PRESS

December ... ...

Hope, like faith, is nothing if it is not
courageous; it is nothing if it is not
ridiculous.

~ Thornton Wilder

ELASTICITY

It's the squeeze and stretch
of a balloon, just shy of popping,
the point of stress that, if not exceeded,
a thing can still return to its original
shape…
        a body bent backwards
without breaking…
            the g-forces
a pilot can withstand… and still
land the plane.
More specifically,
          "the amount
of energy per unit volume that
a material absorbs when
subjected to strain."

A million and a half
deaths now… across
all the continents, here
in the hindsight of 2020…
and that's from Covid alone.

And so, what will be the new
gravitational constant—from
the weight of the three to five

times as many broken hearts,
left to roam the halls of 2021?

And with much more to come,
before the needle of salvation…
will we prove to be elastic enough
to spring back with the bluebonnets
and April blossoms of a desert cactus?

Well… while we wait for an answer…
one poet suggests, as only a poet can:

> Though giant rains put out the sun,
>   Here stand I for a sign.
> Though Earth be filled with waters dark,
>   My cup is filled with wine.

And, as the poet goes on,
as a poet is prone to do:

> Tell to the trembling priests that here
>   Under the deluge rod,
> One nameless, tattered, broken man
>   Stood up and drank to God.

("The Deluge" by G.K. Chesterton)

DHARMA DECORATIONS

~ for Danna Primm
Wednesday, December 2

blue… white… red… green… yellow—
sky and space… air and wind…
fire… water… earth…

tattered prayers unfurled
to the Oklahoma winter winds
high on the Himalaya of her porch,

a string of things designed to fray,
each unwoven thread, a fading
sutra sent off on the breeze

to seed the barren end
of 2020 with good will,
peace, and compassion,

flags and blessings hung
among Christmas lights,
flaming jewels that gleam

in the season of celebrating
a baby God, because father
God has now grown distant

from dealing with needy
and disgruntled followers
who nag, more than pray,

which is why the Buddha
suggests that we all let go
of craving and clinging…

like we will have to let go
of this year by the grace
of every divine being

and holy discipline
we can fit into our lives,
and onto our front porches.

RECURRING

It's official…
Covid has invaded
my subtle nightmares…
dullish, almost nightly, affairs
that no degree of preemptive prayer
seems to be able to prevent or assuage.

It's always an unfamiliar campus—
long a dependable source for bad,
to terrifying, dreams for me—
but now, less about being
unprepared, or naked,
for teaching, and more
about needing to get from
one end of campus to another.

And, like an unnerving video game,
none of the students are wearing masks.
I'm forced to go in some building in order
to get to this other, because I'm late,
despite not knowing what for…
then, there they are, milling
about, the phone-zombies,
sniffling and Tik Tokking
their red-eyed lives away.

Not a one of them adding,
subtracting, or cracking
a philosophy textbook.

And when I backtrack,
a new building appears,
as if constructed while
I was hesitating over in
those rhetorical halls of
the English Department,
and it shines, in chromic,
fluorescent, linoleum-
paved antisepsis.

My therapist says,
recovering from 2020
will require a few decades,
if not a century, of patience,
and a whole lot of goal-setting.
(Not to mention dream analysis.)
But, it will take me even longer
to work my way through
my apparent failure
to teach my dear
little undergrads
a   damn   thing.

Hold On

~ for Jody Karr
Friday, December 4

Due to an unprecedented number
of calls, we are all still waiting
for a representative, sitting
in a cubicle, somewhere
in the poorly-lit offices
of the Year of 2020
to answer the phone.

And it's December, folks.

For concerns about Covid-19,
    please press 1

For worries about when the movers
are going to arrive at the White House
    please press 2

For problems with political partisanship,
    you can press 3,
    but don't expect change

For wishes that the doubters will wise up,
mask up, and do what's best for others,
    go ahead and press 4,

if you think it will help

For questions about the American
medical system, health insurance,
or lack of resources and support
for its workers, or how to fix it,
 5 connects the caller to
 a recorded message
 from Congress

For fears about the planet,
plants, animals, endangered
species, climate, food, water,
 please, please press 6…
 and keep pressing it.
 Do not give up.

For when it will be
safe to go outside again
and try to rebuild our lives,
 press 7… or 8… or 9…
 nobody really knows.

And please do not bother
with zero. It goes nowhere.

To speak to a representative,

please hold on.

Really…
we mean it…
hold on…

hang in there…
with everything you've got…

and the force will be with you, soon.

INERTIA

Even in a vaccinated world…
what would I bounce back to?

Will I hit the vapor trails over
the Atlantic, or that blacktop
weave through all the states,
with a guitar and haversack
full of poems on climate
and cleaning up the air?

Will I continue to order
protein bars and rolled
oats, unscented votive
candles, or Micron pens
online—all that cardboard
and bubble-wrap sticking out
the top of the blue recycle bin—
one of many lies we tell ourselves?

Will I keep Covid happy hour
at 4:00 pm-ish to midnight
and seven days a week?

Will I be a better father
and go see my daughter

for a few days, instead of a few
hours here and there, in between
the road trips I mentioned earlier?

Or will the property of my body,
    proportional to its increasing
        mass, by virtue continue
            in this state of rest,
                in the absence
                of any or all
                    external
                    force?

I'VE BEEN GOOD

~ for St. Nicholas
Sunday, December 6

Thank God for colorful legends
based on untrustworthy biographies.
Because, I don't know what I would do
if Santa Clause, after this long year,
were not coming to my town…

the generous saint, renowned
philanthropist, and general do-
gooder, tossing three bags of gold
into a house to save three daughters
from prostitution…
                              the patron saint
of prisoners and storm-beset sailors,
but, most of all, the children…

Sinterklaas… The Good Saint…
who brought us, by way of good ol'
Dutch ingenuity, the annual tradition of
having to figure out what in the world
a modern materialist doesn't already
have stashed in a closet somewhere.

Santa Claus, based on the Norse god
of thunder, Thor, but associated with

winter and the Yule log, that big chunk
of trunk that burned all through the night.

O, what would we do without that noise,
that clattering, up on the roof, even if
that sleigh was originally a chariot,
and even if those reindeer were
two goats named Cracker
and Gnasher…

I don't care…
I need something here…
at the end of this apoplectic year…

something like an overfed god of a saint,
in his bursting red suit and polished
black boots, cupping his white-
gloved hands, and bellowing
down through the creosote
buildup in the chimney…

"Happy Christmas to all,
and to all a good night!"

WHAT WE CAN DO

~ for my relatives who voted for Trump
Monday, December 7

This bond between us,
we should not ignore.

It signifies the thread
humanity now hangs by.

What saddens me is how similar
we are, and how seldom we consider

the things that make us so: our children,
food on their table, disdain for politicians.

I don't hate Trump quite as much
as I do those deafening tweets

and delirious efforts he made
to tear us even farther apart...

the way a de-arranged child deals
with parental abuse on a playground.

He may talk like you at his big-top rallies,
but a man wearing 12,000 dollar's-worth

of a suit and shoes is constitutionally
incapable of caring about our type.

And, despite all the ways he
reminds us of TV shows

that allow us to feel better
about ourselves by comparison,

we should never forget that we still
have plenty of room for improvement.

And maybe one place to begin would be
to put him well, and firmly, behind us.

A favor that, I promise you,
he'll undoubtedly return.

BRINGING IT HOME

~ for breadwinners
Tuesday, December 8

Because you've got kids
and therefore no choice.

Or because computers run
the whole company anyway
and your office never needed
you behind a desk to begin with.

Because you decided, so long ago,
to work with animals, not people.

Or because you were country
when country wasn't cool,
such an old, old song.

Because you're essential
and therefore didn't have
the luxury of saying "No."

Or because you have always
put the needs of loved ones
in front of your own, and so,
a pandemic won't change that.

For those of you who kept
your eyes steadfast there
on that distant horizon,

even when it stayed dark,
even when it disappeared,
and got your jobs done…

we are aware how this year
didn't pan out for everyone.

So we want to lower our hats
firmly down over our hearts
and offer our severe thanks.

Burnin' the Yule Log at Both Ends

~ for Hallmark
Wednesday, December 9

You may work all twelve months,
but you make your living
off of Christmas
and snow-covered
villages or small towns
ever-encroached-upon by
soulless, big-city corporations,
that miraculously and only in your
one recyclable plot, seem to lose at
their one predictable mission, or…
even more miraculous… are also
converted into loving disciples
of the unprofitable Mom-
and-Pop coffee shop
or over-decorated
little country inn
that celebrates Santa
and his angels year-round,
which, let's face it, is precisely
what you wish you could do too,
because your stock would so rock
the market, if only you weren't still
some private, family-run business
somewhere back in Kansas City,

because, face it, if you
were traded on Wall Street,
the irony would be even more
than your loyal fans could stand,
and they would never want another
cup of hot cocoa in a reindeer mug
ever again, which breaks the heart
just to think about, so, let's not
and spike the eggnog, which
is something I'm very sure
you would never allow,
because your striking
cast always appears
to be terribly sober,
which, I suppose, is
good for your specific
demographic… but…
anyway… I'm just sayin',
if the template ain't broke,
why fix the worn-out thing?

AS LONG AS IT TAKES

~ for Gemma, our foster dog, and WAG
(Wimberley Adoption Group & Rescue)
Thursday, December 10

We drove her home,
and carried her inside,
a 35-pound duffle bag
of raw nerves and bad
wiring, strung by some
slumped over hominid
that never did make it
to staggering around
in an upright position.

Whatever did it to her,
and however it was done,
it was not your everyday
doing of acute damage.
No… a monster lurks
behind this remaining
shadow of sweetness.

So we squat and pet her,
with as much of an angelic
gentleness as we can muster,
while she plays dead in hopes
we won't notice her breathing.

Four days in, her tail now makes
occasional appearances, as she
sniffs out the huge backyard
she's figuring out is all hers.

She's looking in at me, as
I write this, now and then
looking back out at her there,
through a wide-open screen door,

as she runs the necessary calculations
on what a new life might look like...

MY OLDEST FRIEND

~ for Dr. Tim Zeddies
Friday, December 11

We take turns at loneliness,
in our lives so full of people…

sometimes his, sometimes hers…
sometimes yours, very often mine.

I have been exceptional at it all my life.
I remember being lonely in kindergarten,
my favorite moment always being naptime,
when the lights were dimmed and things got
quiet, finally. And during recess, I would bolt
for the creek at a far end of the playground
that lined a golf course—one way home
I was constantly in trouble for taking.
And I still do not understand why.
It had seemed, to me, so natural.

In my teens, I spent unchecked
hours in the canopied arms of an elm
at another edge of that same playground.

To say that I've never needed anybody
may or may not sound true to you…
but I can say, it sure felt that way.

Loneliness has been a spiritual practice
for me. Maybe the world's least attractive
religion. I did not choose it… it chose me.
And, I attend that church even in marriage.

So as the year closes, and the world is still
at an arm's length or three, and hugging
still feels dangerous, and we are still
holding Happy Hour outdoors,
even in the winter's chill…

(and I would be just as happy
holding that hour with myself)

I see now that I have graduated.

I'm a monk… a desert father…
a whirling dervish… spinning
in dizzy circles of loneliness,

should you want any advice.

Where Did I Go?

~ for Karen Zundel
Saturday, December 12

I had to meet myself
all over again this year…
after decades spent in front
of a microphone, reading eyes
in realtime, knowing when a ball
is rolling, points are being scored,
or when the wheel is square and
this thing is going nowhere…

as an audience will make clear
when you're leaning too hard
into that old graduate degree
with its Jacques Lacans, or,
worse, its Stanley Fishes—
I'm well-versed in the face
that is losing all interest.

But now that my crowd
is the rubbery backside
of my smartphone, and
the cedars, the stones…
the bottles and the bones
piled about in pagan altars
on a lot next to our house,

I've had to really get to know
the passionately morose and
chatty recluse of a teenager
who brought me to this life.

The one who played guitar
in total darkness, huddled
on his frameless mattress
in the floor of his room
among relentless hours
of unrequited angst.

I would ask him, So,
what was that about?
The walls… the shaded
windows, and those vinyl
John Denver LPs spinning
and popping into the night?

And, how was that enough
for you, for the seven years
with double ee's at the end?
And when did we lose track
of each other, my old friend?

And, could you show me…
once again… how it works?

RECONNECTING THE FADING DOTS

~ for Karen Zundel
Sunday, December 13

We stave the loss of memory
from the leaky cask of our dry
and cracking brainpans through
every occasion we have to gather
with other dry, cracked brainpans
that were present, back at the time.

Like the one smiling, just to the right
of the Waverly School sign… there,
in the black and white photograph
of that first grade class: '55 – '56.
A sepia reminder of the 55 years
it's been since he moved away
in the middle of the 9th grade.

Yes, a plaid tie like that one
is pretty darn hard to forget.
And, how you reconnected
is as amazing as it is baffling.

Then, you have the daughters
of those two sisters your mom
was friends with in high school
in the 1940s, standing here now,

in your kitchen, having just met
all three of them only weeks ago.

Yes, a collective memory like this
is downright dangerous for both
sets of parents, who aren't able
to defend themselves anymore.

And so it is, as we travel down
the backroads we left to dust,

it's not the growing old itself
that eats away at all of those
yesterdays and long-agos…

it's the growing old alone
that does in the memory.

Raise Your Glasses

~ in memory of Robert Dippo, 1929 to 2020
Monday, December 14

Born and raised
over on the Iowa side
of the Mighty Mississippi...
he helped the Clinton River Kings
to take the State Championship—
enough to hitch a ride on the Tulsa
Golden Hurricane as a nose guard.

A life in law put him on the move—
from the soupy bayous of Louisiana
to Colorado's San Juan mountains...
from the court houses of Wyoming
back over to the Big Apple... even
down to the Cape of Good Hope
up to a bobsled in Switzerland—
one wild ride in a funnel of ice.

A love for the world and travel
that he couldn't possibly not
share with seven children
and his wife of 57 years,
a love big enough for all,
even twelve grandchildren,
not to mention ten greats...

like the love for his Hawkeyes
and Buffs, and that Hurricane…

or a love for a Manhattan on rocks
to go with some good clam chowder,
and an expansive view of the Atlantic…

as well as a love for Benny Goodman's
clarinet, or Glenn Miller's trombone…

a love so big… and a soul so wide…
he was planning a blowout party
for that entire kin and clan
from a hospital bed…

that body so tough,
and a being so true…

it took all of his 91 years,
and a worldwide pandemic,
on this 1st of December,

to finally bring him
home to rest.

HERS WAS A DOG

~ for Ashley, and Cayenne
Tuesday, December 15

There are the quieter losses
we keep mostly to ourselves.
2020 will forbid absolutely any
boasting when it comes to grief.

So she walks over, by herself,
to the Spirit Garden, among
our stone walls, with tears,
a candle, and headphones.

She says her ongoing goodbye
with the cat on her lap, because
he is not done with this either.
And together… they mourn.

All around them, the hours
are falling like leaves down
towards the longest night
we have had in a century,

one that will soon arrive
on this annual abbreviation
when we toast the returning
of light and those longer days.

And she really needs it, as do
all of us, during these darkest
hours of this torrential season,
one we'll not need to see again.

LET'S TRY IT AGAIN

~ for the Grinch
Wednesday, December 16

The mistake was in believing
a heart could grow three sizes
and then would stay that way,
all inflated, from that time on.

Turns out, that dark and jagged,
lonely cave atop a cold mountain,
has been home for so long now,
it's an easy thing to return to…

comfort and familiarity, after all,
gave birth to Newton's first law:
that a body eating chips on a couch
tends not to rise or change its ways.

And so, every year, since 1957, you
go back to resenting the happiness
of others, and have to learn, again,
why those Whos in Whoville sing.

And every year, since I was born,
in '65, I've seen in you the example
of someone who keeps on keepin' on
and returns, time after time, to share

in the Who-pudding, and even carve
the roast beast around the Who-table,
allowing Little Cindy Lou Who yet one
more chance to heal a shriveled heart.

WHATEVER IT TAKES

~ for Terri Stubblefield and Bill Shope,
in memory of Herman L. Hughes
Thursday, December 17

The difference often comes down
to the ones who step in for
the ones who step out.

Dad leaves the family
when you're kids, and
suddenly, it seems like
you have the first single
mother in all of America…
as far as the 60s are concerned.

So, an older brother becomes a man…
and a Granddad comes in, guns blazing,
like a stronger version of John Wayne,
teaches you about grit and how to
hold yourself accountable…

despite your losses…
offers no passes.

A great provider,
as long as you kept
the grades up in math

and English. Tough love,
back before that was a thing.

Tough as the beat-up car he outran
the highway patrolman in—with you
in the front seat watching the compass
bobble and spin on the dashboard…
a thing we would *not* tell Grandma!

The summers wouldn't have been
any nicer with that father in tow.

You fished, you tagged along
on the golf course. A better
grandfather was never had.

So… to ask yourselves, What
would we've done without him?

doesn't get you anywhere… and,
besides, he wouldn't have wanted
for you to bother with it anyway.

PIECED TOGETHER

~ for Susie Clevenger
Friday, December 18

> If your heart is broken,
> make art out of the pieces.
>
> ~ Shane Koyczan

Each piece of a shattered thing
is now a new little wholeness
on its way to being a part
of another something
the world craves.

The ultimate
medium of art
may just be glue.

Every uneven seam…
a stroke of our suffering…
proof of what can be rejoined…
and that perfection has never mattered.

A good long look at the Earth shows
that God doesn't like straight lines.

The reason religion has always

disappointed him, terribly.

And, what are we…
except clods of dirt
and some bone taken
from the broken ribcage
of another's incompleteness?

Next Year, Maybe

~ for Susie Clevenger
Saturday, December 19

Maybe next year
we will be able to gather,
under a sliver of the Snow Moon,
and sing the pieces of our lives
back together again, into
a charming new mess
of chips and shards.

Maybe next year
we'll know better
what it means to be
connected... to sense
that breath on the neck
of an abundance of hugs
now no longer forbidden.

And... maybe next year
we will have a bird's eye
on what will never come
of distrust and division...
remembering it never has.

It could even be, next year,
that some of the little bones

splintered in our hobbled hearts
will fuse and heal, stronger now,
enough to help us bear the other
parts that need some more time.

And, let us hope for next year
to find most folks wrapped up
in the warm bonds that often
seem to form in the throes
of all great recoverings…

as the hammers swing
in a great rebuilding.

SOLSTICE 2020

The sun comes almost
all the way in to the back
wall of the library through
the south windows today.

Its light is at a low point,
a sharp angle at the end
of a year of low points,
and enough sharp angles
to leave a bloody mark…

which is why the softness
of its glow is so surprising.

I cannot take my eyes off
the bands of it humming
across the wood floor…

like a soft-voiced angel
beckoning me to step
forward… toward
better days.

ABLAZE

~ for Vice President Kamala Harris
Monday, December 21

I come to you on no particularly
newsworthy day, because…
I don't want it to color
what I'd like to say.
And that is, you have
stepped in it now. And,
I am also terribly grateful,
for your willingness to do so.
There's no iota of politics behind
what I'm claiming here. I am, instead,
speaking for the daughters of the world.

You have lit a strange new fire, one that
is burning its way through the piles
of all that was once impossible,
fiction finally becoming fact.
So, when I say their eyes
are on you… I intend for it
to haunt your dreams, to disturb
your sleep… and even wakeful hours.
Some people are born for certain moments.
And, some moments are more difficult
than others. You picked a winner.
But I, and they, are with you.

Go Long!

~ for Kellye Hancock,
in memory of David Gentiles
Tuesday, December 22

Eleven years ago,
right about this time,
I wrote, in a brief letter
to another good friend who
had also just died, that you were

> one of the only youth ministers I ever
> liked—who worked at one of the only
> churches I'm still able to step inside
> without feeling I might have eaten some
> bad mayonnaise the night before—

and both of those things are still true.

A mutual friend of ours—who had
known you much better, and who
is still alive—told me that you were

> one of the best human beings he'd
> known. Greeted the world with open
> arms. No judgment, just love. A laugh
> that started about ten feet underground
> and came up through his whole body.

I recall that about you too.

That, and your adamant care
and support for those who had
little to no one else to do the job,
like your undying love and loyalty
for and to the Cleveland Indians...

them, and hundreds of teenagers
who had no desire to grow up...
because of the adults they knew.

You knew how to break bread,
grab that dinner roll of Christ,
and tell them to *Go long!* for it.

And though I do miss you, man,
I'm not sure that your severe case
of empathy would have survived
a Donald Trump *and* a pandemic.

You would have worked yourself
to death to fill the chasm of idiocy
and casualties with some decency
and a mobile Intensive Care Unit
that, for some offhanded reason,
I imagine you throwing together.

And, since you were such a fan
of John Denver, our friendship
was sealed, and unquestioned.

That's why I wrote, at the end
of that letter to my late friend,

> you two burned hot amidst the
> cool of the 21st Century's zoned-out
> mediocrity—this wasteland of smart
> phones, bubblegum, and reality tele-
> vision. You were heavy weights on
> the battered scales of what matters
> in this world.

I TRIPLE-DOG DARE YOU

~ for Ralphie Parker
Wednesday, December 23

You make me nostalgic
for a town that doesn't exist
in the northwest tip of Indiana,
and for a decade I did not exist in.
Something about your blond helmet
and those big tortoise-rimmed glasses
yank at my gut-strings. I ache, again,
for that Red Ryder Carbine Action
200-shot Range Model air rifle…
a source of some of my happiest
early memories… and one sad.
It might be your superhuman
penchant for daydreaming…
another trait that bonds us.
But it's definitely the bully
and jerkwad, Scut Farkus,
who I never one day had
the wherewithal to finally
beat the bloodsnot out of.
Anyway, just keep bringing
what you bring here, to this
beautiful season every year.

Hard to Beat

~ in memory of Jim Chastain
Thursday, December 24

You're the only friend
I ever wrote a book about—
and you had to die for me to do it.
Eleven years ago, to the very day,
it describes when I got the call…

> after a cold wet rain in the night
> that turned to sleet as the morning
> huddled under a gray blanket and
> coughed on the windows…

I'm sitting at the same little red table,
splattered with black and white paint,
like a tiny Pollock canvas, that I sat at
to write those lines, just in a different
room, in a different house, one state
below, with very different weather.

But you weren't merely a friend…
you were a travel mate and fellow
troubadour… and, since I travel
best alone and have a hard time
tolerating poets, that says a lot.

It's come to my attention,
with prodding from my wife,
that I need more good friends
than one who slipped away from
the world, and me, a decade ago.

She's too often right to ignore…
so here in the soft morning light
of early winter, I'm thinking of
what resilience might look like,
if I make the finish line of 2020.

And I sure could use someone
to talk to about this situation.

But the problem is, my man,
you set the bar so damn high.

A LARGE GATHERING

Nobody but me
and Charlie Brown
here this fine morning.
And… by Charlie Brown,
I mean, Vince Guaraldi Trio
slow-jazzing "O Tannenbaum."
Well, then there's Poppin' Fresh,
the Pillsbury Doughboy… who
put the orange roll on my plate.
And hey, so "Linus and Lucy"
just showed up, bearing one
of the great piano riffs ever.
Anyone who hears that song…
and doesn't smile? probably has
mom issues and votes republican.
Anyway, it appears Ashley is up,
since I can see Ralphie on TBS
in the living room, saying "Ooh
fuuuuudge…" Only he didn't say
"fudge." He said THE word, the big
one, the queen-mother of dirty words.
The point at which I had to step out
into the backyard and ease tensions
between the foster dog and two cats.

It's a huge yard, and each wants it all.
Like Charlie Brown's little sister, Sally.
All they want is what they have coming
to them. All they want is their fair share.
Which has been one of the drawbacks
of a holiday bogarted by capitalism...
but look, the sun's out and shining.
It's a toe-pinching 53°. The coffee
is hot and spiked with a little nog.
The construction crew has the day
off from the lots across the street,
and my seasonal gang is all here,
virtually distanced, each playing
the role we've played every year
for the years I care to remember.

And so we would like to wish you
a Merry Chris-Hanu-Kwanzaa...
and a Happy-Please-Dear-God-
or-Whatever-You-Believe-in-
to-Beg-for-Covid-Mercy...

New. Year.

ASSUME LIFE

~ for Luri Owen
Saturday, December 26

Let's say some survive.
Let's say we make it to be
one of those who someday
avails children or, maybe,
the children of children,
of the Great Pandemic
way back in 20 of 20:
O, I remember it well.
You know, those types.
Those who begin stories
woefully shaking heads.

Yes, for some of us…
we must assume life…
that some new variation
of it will continue on…
with terrible absences.

The father of my father
was a gritty by-product
of the Dust Bowl days,
out in west Oklahoma.
He preferred bananas
that were past prime,

54

and he didn't talk much.
He worked in the stench
of a huffing oil refinery
he was known to say
smelled like bread
and butter to him.
It took my first job
cleaning the burned
crust of chicken skin
off dented oven pans
in the musty basement
kitchen of dad's church
to see what he'd meant.

Grandma grew the okra
and jarred the plum jelly.
And there were no means
to no end where the trains
carried all the wealth away
to St. Louis and San Fran.
They had little to speak of.
And, some days, nothing.
But, they never assumed
death. They just figured
there'd come a next year,
and that they would live it,
when it got around to them.

Out Past and Beyond

~ for Mike Bumgarner
Sunday, December 27

The problem with perfect childhoods—
whether Wichita Falls, in Texas, or
up in Norman, Oklahoma—
where we ruled our little
neighborhood kingdoms,
roamed them on bike-back
and shared mothers, moms
who always seemed to have
enough bologna and bread,
no matter how many of us
punks showed for lunch—

is that they do little to nothing
to prepare us for the way a world,
out past those wind-rattled, sun-
bleached stop signs, is going to
really operate, once we venture
out there, where we no longer
know the cracks in the sidewalk.

That's why we spend the rest of our
grown-up lives coming from behind,
as we enter the job scene and the race
for constant professional advancement.

We remember those days, the ones
before texting, posting, and next-
day shipping, and we can't figure
why no one out here understands
how they made for better politics
and more bipartisan relationships.

But, eventually, the sight of pain
and confusion in the earnest eyes
of our only daughters, forges us
into men, and we either break,
or we devote all we have left
to improving their odds...

out beyond the signs
they grew up with.

In or Out

~ for Larry Smith
Monday, December 28

Billy Collins tells me his poems
come from a mouse that stands
on his shoulder and whispers
odd things into his ear…

and I said 'odd.'
He did not.

But, it's true
that the better
poets are out of
their minds, while
they write, and mice
are as good as anything
to blame our condition on.

And let me tell you, steer clear
of those poets who write inside
their minds. Whew! — They will
wear you out like a set of bagpipes
blasting and wheezing in the kitchen.

Sort of like poets who leave their minds
altogether, and never come back to visit.

They sprinkle words sparsely all over
the page, and then back away…
slowly, into the shadows…
waiting for you to get
what isn't there.

No, the good poems
are a conniving invitation
to the reader to leave her own
mind for a little while, to listen to
her own mouse whispering in her ear
that the mind isn't all it's made out to be.

My Self, and I

~ for Larry Smith
Tuesday, December 29

It took me a long time
to really dig my self...
to finally grok it... if
you get what I mean.

On that mystical day,
I guess, I figured out
no one else was going
to do this for me first.

I don't recall the date,
but I was likely sitting
in a tree, on a beach,
by, say, Carmel Bay...
(I have had numerous
revelations in that very
cypress tree, just above
the white-feather sand.)

In those wasted years
before I dug my self,
because, well, sadly,
I didn't believe in it,
I would crawl up in

to my moody mind, which
is the best place to avoid
and get away from your
self.

O, I would spend
days at a time up there
wondering why no one
else seemed to dig me.
And, my mind would
explain it all away—
which is, apparently,
what minds do best.

But, ultimately, I got
tired of listening to it,
like any frumpy expert
in any fallacious field,
and so, after extensive
deliberations between
my mind and a long-
ago distanced self...

that self, and I, came
to the conclusion that
it was now time for us
to go out of our mind.

WHAT I HEAR IN YOU

~ for Sierra Brown
Wednesday, December 30

If the movie of our life
had a soundtrack playing
in its background, the times
we'd spent together would be
some mix of *A Charlie Brown
Christmas* and maybe *Edward
Scissorhands*, don't you think?

Road trips would need a touch
of *Spirit: Stallion of the Cimarron*,
but sprinkled with some *Raiders
of the Lost Ark* and John Denver
(I sort of forced him on you…).

All through, Peter Gabriel would
make loud appearances, in which
we'd play air guitars and drums, as
we sang up on some imaginary stage.
(We'd have to pay him royalties for it.)

But the times we spent apart, Honey,
will forever sound to me something
like that earth-shake beach landing
in *Saving Private Ryan*, or the scene

in *The Thin Red Line* when Nick
Nolte replays the burning down
of the village in his dying mind,
or maybe those beautiful strains
of guitar in *Brokeback Mountain*.

But ever and always… Luciano
Pavarotti singing *Nessun dorma*.

Yet, whatever music has been,
what I hear in your voice now
sounds like the opening theme
to *Star Trek: Deep Space Nine*…
man, that overture just kills me.

That, and Coldplay's *Viva la Vida*,"
or *The Final Bell* from the movie *Rocky*,
make me feel how I do when I hear you
sing Matt Denman's *Our Heart's Disease*.
You blew that up like an exploding star.

But even here, at the close of this wild,
nut-bomb year, it's nowhere near time
for the credits to roll on our story.

And a ... New Year

> Of all sound of all bells... most solemn
> and touching is the peal which rings
> out the Old Year.
>> ~ Charles Lamb

I fear we may put
too much pressure
on 2021 to be better
in some way. Just like
we've placed too much
blame on the hunched
shoulders of 2020...

as if it had sentience,
and some darkish will
to devastate our lives...

as if this impending year
might have compassion...

as if Moderna and Pfizer
will save us from having
to face the other, nasty,
dung-covered eggs still
unhatched in our nest.

Just what you wanted
to hear, right? A poet's
cup o' cheer, to usher in
a long-awaited new year?

So… forget those poets…
but just for this one night…

and raise up your salty glasses,
or bubbly if you must, and toast
those solemn and touching bells
that will ring out the Old Year,

then peal in the new, with all
its hopes and hardships…
promises… pressures…
dreams and… well…

whatever it takes.

January ... ...

My country freed itself from one evil.
I wish another liberation would follow.

~ Adam Zagajewski

New Years' Days

The Roman god, Janus,
had two faces, and gave
this month its name…
two faces that looked
in opposite directions,
one to peer back over
last year's hot messes,
that other with eyes up
ahead, focused, we hope,
on how to clean things up.

On this day—the seventh
of Christmas, and the first
of a year—an 18th-Century
poet laureate was expected
to compose, and to deliver,
an ode for the royal family.

Colley Cibber's were known
to be so bad, they made even
18th-Century eyes roll upward,
before dropping to the ground.

My signal to stop this one now.
A signal poets too often ignore.

In the 19th Century, the character
of the first person to set a foot
in your house after midnight,
also set the tone for the year.

And this time around, for us,
I am afraid the character was
me, after taking out the trash.

Some years you win, some…

Anyway, thank goodness
the 20th Century came
to divest us of every
old superstition—

so that, in 1999,
we could go ahead
and party like it was.

The problem being, we had
no superstitions now to instill
moderation and, therefore,
the party never ended,

which brought on…
the big bully of 2020,

whom so many of us continue
to pick fights with, to varying
degrees of failure.

And so it is
that this, the first day of 2021,
has me thinking.

About what…
I don't know, yet.
I'll get back to you.

Given Four Choices

~ for Patrick Marshall
Saturday, January 2

To the accountant made mad
by distance and destinations,
a crossroads is only a minor
ingredient in a prescription,
a factor in the equation of
departures and arrivals.

To the seasoned traveler,
who is savvy enough now
to leave lots of extra time,
a crossroads is brimming
with helpful alternatives
to a traffic-infested city
that lies straight ahead.

To one with no home,
some nomad wandering
the backstreets and alleys
of a hostile and intolerant
society, a crossroads can
be the difference between
a warm spot or frozen toes,
a soup kitchen… or that first

cousin who won't be glad
to see you at the door.

To the indecisive…
a crossroads is Hell.

To the lost… it's equal
parts hope and despair.

And, to a poet… it will
remain the bothersome
metaphor that haunts
his every endeavor.

WE ARE GATHERED

~ for Anne Roberts
Sunday, January 3

As we gather 'round a fire tonight,
from the Texas Hills to Indiana,
a fine state that will someday
have to change its name…

I am holding onto me…
those parts that came off
the axels about the middle
of March and on into April.

From the Bronx to Southern
Pennsylvania, or Wisconsin on
to the lower coast of Oregon,
I'm also holding onto you…

those huddled under quilts
here, in the winter of our
descent into new variants
and a Phase 3 Lockdown.

From San Luis Obispo, CA
to Guilford, CT, I have heard
that some of you are holding
onto each other now as well.

And some are even re-holding
after many years of letting go…
stories of electric reconnections
that are resoldering my sad wires.

So, from your memories of Tonga
flown back to Port Arthur, Texas…
or from your deserts of Saudi Arabia
back home to Shawnee, Oklahoma…

hold onto yourselves, and to each other.
And if you have a little holding left over,
hold onto me too. For the day is coming
when we'll feel the fire we gather 'round.

BETTER DIRECTIONS

~ for Mike Bumgarner, from Celia Jones
Monday, January 4

As a minister, a leader,
back in my college days
at my father's church, you
were the boss, and a friend.

You were that mildly crazy one
who didn't drive me more crazy
than I was going and, therefore,
didn't push me all the way away

from God—which was the way
I was headed. You took on my
blasphemies with a big shrug
and a sly grin, hand on back.

As a boss, when I graduated
to college leader myself, you
were a friend, and a minister
to my growing set of wounds.

Wounds you helped me doctor
by exposing your own… much
deeper ones. More painful ones
that you never used to shame me.

Down a long road, as my friend,
you taught me that a good boss
is just a guide, along life's ways,
who points in better directions.

And that the world has never
needed its ministers more…
the job that I'm still working,
off at some necessary distance.

Which, it turns out, is the thing
I had been looking for all along.
A thing you'd sort of pointed at,
without ever really saying a word.

Then Sings My Soul

~ in memory of my aunt, Bettye Lou Kennedy
Tuesday, January 5

The measure of a soul
requires a lot of tools
and multiple readings.

The depths of wisdom
and the heights of basic
common sense are givens.

But when we begin to gauge
the soul's capacity to outright
laugh until tears, and a sudden
silence, are all we have to go on,
that she is indeed enjoying herself,
the portrait takes on an added glow.

And when one is known to be sweet
and gentle, with a loving touch,
yet prone to episodes of
pixie-like prankery...
all mixed up and in
with a solid hankering
for solitaire or gin rummy...
we know the life wasn't boring.

After all is said and measured,
though, it's the subtleties, things
that do not register on the meters
and scales, that we need to go by.

Like the capacity to sit on a patio
at sunset, sipping on a white zin,
and singing, softly to one's self,

> *Then sings my soul,*
> *my Savior God to Thee*
>
> *How great Thou art,*
> *how great Thou art.*

TALL IN THE SADDLE

~ for Ron Wallace
Wednesday, January 6

You don't lasso God,
put a bit in his mouth,
then throw a saddle on
believing you can now
lead him wherever you
think he ought to go...
for instance, to water
(where you would also
not be able to make him
drink), much less the well
of a Baptist-spun theology.
He never once recommended
denominations as a reservation
system for the pasture of heaven.

No... God is the cowboy, my friend.
And you're just another pear cactus
that constitutes the thorny reason
he likes to wear those buckaroos.
And when it gets down to who
he lets through that rusty old
pipe-rail gate there at the ass
end of that Last Big Day...
you're likely in for a shock.

CRUX

~ for Danna Primm, Jeanne Fell, and Celia Jones
Thursday, January 7

It took one, truly ugly, night
(years ago, in New Mexico)
for the disease of my anger
to crystalize into something
I could see for what it was.
Just enough of something
that I could, finally, verify
its existence, and ugliness,
and so determine that this
should not be my legacy.
And, it was the presence
of my daughter to witness
it, compounding my shame,
that generated enough energy
to ignite the forces for change.

Yesterday afternoon, on the Day
of Epiphany, the United States
got the chance to see, severely
and clearly, what it is not above.

We now know, from image after
live-rolling, then endlessly-looping,

image—what is also not below us...
and the depths we'll go to to show it.

When a grown man with a full beard,
who hasn't washed socks in months,
storms the capitol with another man
wearing the pale red cape of a failed
president, and waving a desecrated
flag—neither of them believing in
the history of proven bad ideas—
we become a cartoon we deserve.

Because, somewhere around 200-
million good, hard-working people
will never make for breaking news.
There's just no eye-popping footage.

Because, the rest of the world knows
what it wants to see. And that is it—
what happened in the hollowed halls,
teargas chambers, shattered windows,
and infiltrated offices, up on The Hill,
around 6:30 pm Greenwich Mean Time.
The time that will mark whether, or not,
this nation has the gumption to change.

TRUMPLANDIA

Thursday, January 7

I'm talking of a new continent.
One that we'd manufacture, if
we had to.
       And one that floats.
As long as prevailing currents
carry it away—possibly even
in a new direction—a new
point on the compass—one
we're never able to locate again,
once arrangements are finalized…
and the drifting's done its holy work.

There will be a glorious isolation for all…
well, for Trump and all who voted for him,
a second time. He will serve as their Holy-
Dictator-and-Demagogue-in-Chief-His-
Excellency-President-for-Life-Field-
Marshal-Al-Hadji-Doctor-Donald-
Trump-Dada-VC-DSO-MC-CBE-
Lord-of-All-the-Beasts-of-the-Earth-
and-Fishes-of-the-Seas-and-Conqueror-
of-the-British-Empire-in-General-and-
Trumplandia-in-Particular in perpetuity,
anon, and on, forever and ever… amen.

What a delirious new nation it will be…
once it's finally sucked into a wormhole
opened up by anonymous imageboards
that post holographic disinformation.

Hell, it's almost enough to make
a sane man wanna renounce
his U.S. citizenship.

THESE REMAIN

~ on the insurrection of January 6, 2021,
a dark day near the end of dark years
Friday, January 8

Faith is a bruised and dead-tired
private, hovering over the body
of a fallen friend… one soldier
who will go on, determined now
to honor the memory of the lost.

Hope is a wounded, and rattled,
captain, looking through smoke
over the battlefield, who would
never leave his troops, to fend
for themselves in what's ahead.

Love is an old general, walking
with a limp from an earlier war,
who knows damn well the awful
consequences for all concerned,
if he ever abandons his charge.

UNVERWÜSTLICH

~ for Christa Pandey,
in honor of Sigrid von Holst
Saturday, January 9

Looking out over the Mighty Rhine
for 91 years… she has seen a lot
of gray history pass by below.

The bombing of Cologne
by the Brits, back in 1943,
around three weeks before
her confirmation ceremony.

The family lost everything…
had to search for another town
that had not been blown into total
unrecognition by the Royal Air Force.

Those twin spires over in Cologne…
or the Beethoven Haus in Bonn…
among few things left looming…
off in a forever-changed distance.

At the other end of the decades,
there was the slow loss of a good
husband… along with the hard
loss of a rather hard daughter.

A broken femur... and the two
hip replacements. God himself
could barely stand much more.

So now, there's the sliding on
of those same three rings...
followed by the short drives
to a nearby village for fruit,
veggies, and bread and then
the drive back to the house
for another day... alone...

and yet, with her steadfast
faith held in the melodies
of "Lobe den Herren" or
"Befiehl du deine Wege,"

"Praise the Almighty" and
"Entrust your way," hymns
to keep a heart strong, holy
lines for holding onto hope.

A hope of singing them again,
soon, in the fellowship of friends.

SORRY TO BOTHER YOU

~ for Saint Jude
Sunday, January 10

As the sky sheds blades of ice
in the Texas hills this morning,
I'm mulling over the vocabulary
of the last four days in the news:

> 25th Amendment
>   impeachment
>   unsound
>   unhinged
> nuclear codes

and feel that it's time to call
upon you, once again, O Patron
of the Impossible... holy overseer
of lost causes and desperate situations.

For, as some other Jude wrote, long ago,
in a very brief letter to the New Testament:

> ...these people slander whatever they do
> not understand, and they are destroyed
> by those things that, like irrational
> animals, they know by instinct.

which, granted, is a slight to most animals.
As a good many animals are more rational
than the humans making headlines today.

He went on to call them "grumblers and
malcontents" who are "bombastic
in speech, flattering people
to their own advantage."

which I find disheartening,
where 2,000 years' worth of
nothin's changed is concerned,
which also must mean, however,
that business is booming for you.

I can almost hear the bleary sighs,
as you heave out of bed to put on
your big slippers and little glasses,
then plop down at the computer
to check the inbox… Whoa!

Anyway, just wanted you
to know we could use all
the help you might throw
our way in these prodigal,
discombobulated months.

LIKE DUCT TAPE

~ for Anne Harris
Monday, January 11

Sometimes family
is a global coordinate,
the latitude and longitude
of a soup tureen in the middle
of a big dining room table in an old
Victorian-style house of depression-era
grandparents in a town like Stroud, America,
along Route 66 in the heartline of Oklahoma.
People we would call grandma 'n' grandpa.

It's like those metal rocking chairs on
the front porch that wraps around,
or the dormer windows on each
side of a cavernous attic filled
with stacks of brown boxes
and waiting books, moth-
balled clothes, and old
National Geographics.

Sometimes family
is the collective echoes
of a screen door slamming,
the cricket-song and cicada-buzz
so loud on summer nights we gave up

on conversation. It's the thunder of those
marbles tossed into the attic fan, by one of
the boys. To this day no one will admit to it.
But also the roar of that fan all night long…
the sound of grandpa saying *Got your nose*,
or *By golly*, or trying to sing, *How much is
that doggie in the window* to the hammers
of the spinet… or, grandma reading
Lucinda the Donkey. But, definitely,
the tick-tock-and-toll of clocks
in the stairwell, or by a fire.

And sometimes family
is those remembered aromas
of pipe smoke on Christmas Day,
or gutted fish just outside the house
from the day's trip to the lake nearby.

And often, it's the savor of hot waffles
from the half-dead iron with the frayed
cord we all worried would someday burn
the place down. And always the homemade
noodles, and hand-cranked peach ice cream,
undercooked bacon, or the oranges, apples,
and that one piece of candy, in the toes
of time-worn Christmas stockings.

And yes, sometimes family is
the touch of running fingers
over our initials, carved in
to that railing, at the top
of the stairs, the pieces
of a puzzle, the puffs
of a pillow ambush.
                    Or,
the stickiness of duct tape
holding threadbare slippers,
even a split potato one time,
together, which, now that we
think about it, feels a lot like
what held this family fast…
duct tape…   and love.

But, forever, family
will be the soft ease
of being together…

our unshakable spirit,
what makes us bigger
than we could ever be
without it, on our own.

The Burden

~ to those who stormed the Capitol
Tuesday, January 12

We each have who we listen to.
Which is never each other.
So I am here to do that.
I have finally learned
that to get what I want…
my mouth has to stop moving.

And what we need to do here
is seldom ever pulled off.
History wearily tells us
we'll kill each other's sons
and daughters for a few decades
before we get tired and sad enough.

Another problem I see would be how
incredibly annoyed I am, already,
with what you're going to say.
But, that is my problem…
and I will have to work
my own way through it.

In the meantime, know this…
screaming obscenities, threatening
my family, and smiting me with a flag

I saw you let drag in the dirt, will not...
change what I believe. Only good reasons.
And, I'm not so sure you have any of those.

Therefore, please do some solid research
before we begin—and QAnon is not
a source. I recommend something
more practical, like looking into
the nature, and the nuances,
of "the burden of proof."

THE DIRTY HALF DOZEN

~ to U.S. representatives Andy Biggs of Arizona,
Michael Cloud of Texas, Marjorie Taylor Greene
of Georgia, Doug Lamalfa of California, Scott
Perry of Pennsylvania, but especially Markwayne
Mullin of Oklahoma
Wednesday, January 13

I want this poem to be
so soft, you barely feel it
when it hits you later on,
after someone tells you
what happens, later on,
at the end of the poem.

And I'll tread so lightly,
here in the beginning,
the likes of the six
of you will stop
reading now,
because the likes
of you have no idea
how poem endings work.

So… let me start by saying,
it was not your smug refusal
to wear masks when crowded
in an undisclosed location with
your fellow U.S. representatives,

as you stood, or sat, with arms folded,
in a snotty air of feigned indifference
to the political nature of your deed.

It was your smiles.

And now that several colleagues
are in quarantine, or the hospital,
keep in the diminishment of your
sickly minds, that if even one
of them dies, you will be,
even if not convicted,
       murderers.

And to the one
from Oklahoma
whose first name
is suspiciously made
of two smashed together…
who said to the lady of Delaware
trying to give him a mask "I'm gonna
come over there and hug you…" You…
my fellow Okie, sound like a serial killer
whose victims are yet to be discovered.

MOST TIMES

~ for those barely hanging on
Thursday, January 14

Whatever you're at the end of,
it's probably not a rope, unless,
you're in the habit of acting out
metaphors, which... suddenly...
sounds sort of interesting to me.

More likely, you're at the end of
your patience. Or, for many of us,
it's money. For some it's empathy,
for others it's our sanity altogether.

The man who created the Land
of Narnia said, "We hold our
mental health by a thread."

If the rope you're at the end of
begins to feel more like a thread,
grab a pen, and some paper too,
with no intention of being a poet
(they're mostly aloof ingrates...
who ruin otherwise fun parties)
then, break the bread of your
feelings into lines and stanzas.

Plant a tree, or a row of flowers.
And with the dirt wedged under
your nails, realize the magnitude
of what you have just done for
the sake of a new generation.

Or find whatever you think
might bring you back from
the brink of your threadbare
emotional mindscape.
                                    Then,
while you're in there, serenade
yourself with this subtle refrain
of a seldom subtle friend of mine,

  'Cause at the end of the rope…
  *there's a little more rope most times.**

And hell, if you happen to have two
ropes, tie them to a solid branch
and make a big swing…
it's never too late.

                          * "Carlisle's Haul"
                          by James McMurtry

BRACING FOR IT

Here in the weekend
before the inauguration,
I am afraid we have some
blue-steel days ahead of us,
aerosolized-bromide months
that will mess with our mucous
membranes of the eyes and nose.

Dark promises are being made, out
in the basements and backwaters,
and the exurbs of our boredom,
in this wavering democracy
built on Whataburger
and Inalienable Rights
for those who are white
and want to believe in wild
web-manufactured delusions.

My guess is that citizens will die,
and I know the type who's already
getting pumped at the prospect of it.
They buy $200 camouflaged jackets,
military-grade black boots, AR-15s,
and Christmas presents for moms,

but none of it fills that dark
and capitalistic void inside.

And so they'll resort to
fratricide—because…
the video games don't
get them off anymore.

Therefore, let us pray…

for that implacable aching
they can never quite assuage…

for those on the receiving end of it…

and for a country that will have to find
a way to house their relentless anger.

Heaven Forbid

But is uniformity of opinion desirable?
No more than of face and stature.

~ Thomas Jefferson

If everyone agreed with me,
I would dislike everyone else
more than I already do. For,
they would possess perfect
knowledge, being privy to
the answers to everything.

And who can stand people
like that? I mean… geez…
it would just wear me out.

Shindigs would be ghastly
affairs, with nothing to do
but stand around and chirp
an endless string of "yeses,"
"mhms," and "I knooows,"
God save us from ourselves.

What I'll Always Remember

Sunday, January 17

No food or drink
for 20 minutes
before the test.
Never a problem,
since that's how long
it takes me to peel back
and open the little packet
with that long cotton swab.

Cough, deeply, 3 times, then
make sure to get the inside of
each cheek, the upper and lower
gums, on top, then beneath, your
tongue, and the roof of the mouth.
All the places we sometimes forget
exist up there in those wetlands.

Insert the sample into the tube.
Do not spill or drink the liquid.
Not something I would've ever
considered without the warning.

Break the swab at the scored line
until you hear that satisfying snap.

Secure the cap. Shake the tube 3 times
to coat the swab in the solution…
knowing now… it is finished.
Your work here is done…
the best you could do it.

Nothing left, except
to zip the thing up
in that biohazard
baggie it came in

and turn it over to
the girl in the kiosk
through the sterilized
metal slot that makes you
think of a checkpoint in East
Berlin, somewhere along a wall.

What's Going On

Santa Fe already has
the Roundhouse and other
state capitol buildings blocked
by flashing lights and heavy fences.

I had to go around on Paseo de Peralta
to get to the house on Loma Encantada.
But I was determined to spend this
week within walking distance
of some capitol… state,
or otherwise. And this
is the only one with a
nice place to spend it,
thanks to sweet friends
who don't have the sense
to keep us poets away from
their very rarefied real estate.

And that's not true. I had no plan
to be near a capitol. I made that up
when I pulled into town and noticed
the police cars everywhere.
                    But…
it sounds ripe for a good story,

and it's usually best if poets
don't know what they are
getting themselves into.

Anyway, I am here now,
journal, pens, and tequila

all at their respective posts
and reporting for duty... sir.

WHITE ON BROWN NONVIOLENCE

Tuesday, January 19

Snow-dusted adobe walls
cure anger. Try it sometime.
You can't look out a window
and see it, the sepia contrast
of that feathery white upon
the horseback brown, and
then think, You know…
I'm gonna turn and slap
the next cheek I see.

It might even be enough
to convince the Proud Boys,
and their brothers in ignorance,
the Nazi skinheads—who believe
turning the other cheek is for sissies
and saviors—to take tomorrow off…
at least here in Santa Fe. Violence is so
mentally and emotionally taxing.
We could all use a break.

As for me, I have decided
to stay in and play with my
pen—semi-automatic pistol
that it is—while enjoying this
view just outside the window.

CAN I CALL YOU THAT?

~ for President Joe Biden, on Inauguration Day
Wednesday, January 20

Dear Joe,

    (I feel like I can
    call you that now…
    it is one of the things
    I appreciate about you.)

I do not envy you though…
mostly because I have spent
my days avoiding what you
have spent yours pursuing.

Yet it creates a balance here
in a time that needs the very
diametric styles of language
we each bring to our chairs
at the rowdy American table.

And may God bless us both
in the herculean days ahead.

But know that I am in service
to what you appear to be as well.
The list of dire necessities you gave

in your inauguration speech read—
item for item—like the one I keep.

And though I worry about your age
somewhat, I have come to believe
that what is grandfatherly in you?
might be our best, or only, chance.
So please, do continue to workout
and eat your leafy green vegetables.
Don't get my hopes up, then fizzle.

All patronizing aside… I will admit
to crying when you took the oath.
Almost as much as I cried when
Kamala took hers—though…
I'm not sure she'd go for this
first-name business we share.
But, I sort of like her too…
she brings a finger-snap to
the boring party of politics.

Maybe I cried for what is,
finally, dear God in heaven,
over.
          But, I know I cried for
a new hope, though it's much
more gossamer than it is giddy.

Anyway, you need to get
onto your executive orders.
And I need to edit this poem
for a little show I have tonight.

Still, I want to thank you, sir,
for this little chat we've had.
That last guy?
          Geez… that
blunderbuss of a gas-bag
blowhard never listened
to a damn word I said.

In a Flash

~ for Sierra Brown, and all daughters,
on the occasion of the inauguration
Thursday, January 21

So, this morning…
I'll toss poetry to the curb
and break its rules of refinement
to come before those who still
read the stuff, as I drop
my metaphorical
shorts, and…
    gush.

There will be no dignity
in doing so, but yesterday

  art kicked hate's ass.

The Marine Band stuck their
frozen Marine lips to trumpets
and played "Hail to the Chief."

Lady Gaga, in a massive pink
skirt the wind tried to steal,
sang the national anthem
with her cords of steel.

And I did not intend
to rhyme those lines.

Garth Brooks sang
"Amazing Grace,"
just after J.Lo did
a Woody Guthrie
tune? Which twists
a neck to think about.

But then Amanda Gorman,
all 22 youngish years of her,
took the podium and dazed
millions of listeners. She
embarrassed the very
etymological foundation
of the term white supremacy.

And she may have even hauled up
poetry from the ash and bone piles
down in the catacombs that thread
below the shrine of literary forms.

But look, Ms. Gorman, I have
written a poem for every day
you have lived, with a thousand
and one to spare. But I'm not bitter.

I was happy for you to take
the gig, that was rightfully
mine.
             And you did call
for unity. So, I'm here
to serve, if need be.

Later in the day,
Bruce Springsteen
took me to the Land
of Hope and Dreams, as

Tim McGraw 'n' Tyler Hubbard
made me want to reconsider
my beliefs about country
music… and its fans.

Hell, Jon damn Bon Jovi
did "Here Comes the Sun"
at the end of a pier out over
the Atlantic to—get this—
a cloud-draped sunrise.

And did I spy the former
President, yes, Barack Obama,
playing lead for the Foo Fighters?

Anyway, something about the Lincoln
Memorial reflecting off the hood
of John Legend's grand piano
got me a bit wet in the eyes.

But when Katy Perry
exploded in white,
from head to toe,
to a huge firework
display, there behind
the Washington Monument,

I jumped up. And I began to dance
and sing like a sixth grader who thinks
no one is watching her. And I wept.

I wept for the blazing power
of artists…
                        and I wept
for a hope flashing
in the darkness.

GOT IT?

~ for Konrad Eek
Friday, January 22

Sometimes resilience
is taking the next breath,
despite the inherent danger.

What lives in the American air
and the history of our lungs
has some dark episodes.

But we've sprinkled it,
liberally, with goodness
and art, tequila and gin,

things we share with our
carefully chosen friends.
That necessary practice.

I have set aside my work
to write one more poem.
Which is what I always do

when bad news comes down
from a brother in art's arms.
I lit a candle, piñon incense,

because prayer makes me nervous,
as a recovering P. K. of the plains.
An old problem I need to get over.

So, this is what you get, my friend.
An old poet who'll never get over
anything happening to the best

of what modicum he has left,
because he never had much
to begin with… meaning…

we are just going to have to
get through whatever this is
to some other side. Capiche?

Upon My Return

~ to the City of Holy Faith
Saturday, January 23

I'm missing Santa Fe while I'm here.
I walk the plaza in a black mask, as if
I'm a terrorist or tourist from Texas,
and almost no one cares to join me,
or even block my well-worn paths.

I pass by old doorways I have had
intimate relations with for decades
and there is a hidden force field
that threatens to zap me, if
I were to fondle one.

The sign behind glass
in the Collected Works
Bookstore fades, and reads:

    Offering Online Orders
    & Curbside Pick Up Only

and I wonder if there's irony
in grabbing poetry, To Go,
in a white Styrofoam box.

I drive by Maria's, slowly,

and worry that Juan might not
make it if I am not in that stool
at the end of that bar asking him
to put my Silver Coin straight up
with salt, to sip with my blue corn
enchiladas smothered in Christmas.

And it's too cold to bother Carlos
on the patio behind Luminaria
for Green Chile Latkes.

The list is as long as
the heartache is wide.
But I'm going to keep it,
here... close to my breast...
and after I get that second shot,
I will blaze a dusty trail back to this
holy town, worn thin by the dreams
of transplanted artists, the foreign
theology of saints, and the cold
resentment of the indigenous,
and I will enter, once again,
each of these pearly gates,
with hunger, thirst, and lust
for life, literature, liquid gold,
liberty, and... most certainly...
red and green chile sauce for all.

T-BONES AND PISTOLS

~ for Paul White
Sunday, January 24

He poured a small toast
of well over 100-proof absinthe,
an opening offering of anise enjoyed
by Picasso and Proust, Hemingway and
that famously depressed poet Baudelaire,
before bringing out the añejo margaritas,
one of which he sipped as he slapped
a couple of T-bones on the grill.

And as the fat began to sizzle
he went indoors to retrieve
the backpack full of pistols
he got off a friend who is dying
of cancer and therefore taking drugs
that render him considerably less safe—

he shot a round into a wall while showing
my friend how beautiful the big .44 was.

So my friend was careful to make sure
the six chambers were empty before
he showed me how beautiful it was.

My friend's sort of decent that way.

My favorite though, had to be
the Ruger Vaquero .357 mag
with the simulated ivory grips.

Man… that baby was easy to lift
and level at arm's length to the eye.

And as I viewed the blue sagebrush
and the cholla cactus over that steel
sight, he brushed on red chile sauce
and flipped the steaks, then patched
the margaritas from that golden bottle.

And that's when I thought how one might
think we were sitting on a back porch
of some shack out on the fringes
of, say, Terlingua, Texas…

instead of a tiny patio
behind some adobe
townhouse out in
the burbs north
and a bit west
of Santa Fe.

THE OTHER END OF THE LINE

~ for those who make death threats
Monday, January 25

A King James version
of the Holy Bible, a black
leather hardback, sits prone
on your coffee table, maybe
with a grandmother's name
on the cover in gold leaf...

with verses she underlined
remaining entirely ignored.

In your dry county, Christ
gets blamed for everything.

And so, you romanticize
the stone of your hatred
and paint it as a mission,

putting your own profane
words in God's mouth...

a dangerous business...
when you haven't had
an intellectual erection
in some 20 to 30 years.

That's why the only love
you have left is to threaten
the lives of those who think,

the last bastion of willful
ignorance out on parade
as a 200-pound toddler
with a beard who didn't
get his way. Poor thing.

A BURNING QUESTION

~ for you, beneath the bridge last night
Tuesday, January 26

When I awoke,
sometime before
6:00 am, my mind
got dressed against
the snow and trudged
down to the bottom end
of Old Taos Highway just
this side of the Post Office
where you were wrapped up
in every layer you've been able
to collect in your shopping cart
for as long as you've known that
winter was coming to the dry-dirt
bed beneath the concrete bridge by
Rosario Boulevard.
                              And, of course,
I forgot to bring you some breakfast,
or better yet, a shot of gold tequila…
the only legal fire in the town limits.
I'm too often thoughtless that way.

My body, still under several layers
in a balmy bedroom up the road,
stayed put and decided to adhere

to an unspoken set of absurd laws
that prohibit me from inviting you
into this wonderful house, that has
enough space for you and ten more.

So… I put the kettle on a burner
and couldn't keep from thinking
how you might enjoy a hot cup,
as well as how I may never feel
the kind of cold you're feeling
right now. My phone says 12°.

And, what good does it do you
for me to sit at this kitchen table
and scribble you out a prayer for
warmth and maybe a decent meal?

I just took off my slim reading glasses
and stared at the oven for five minutes
to contemplate that moot question…

and… the only thing I came up with
was that not to do so would amount
to yet one more sin I'd have to add
to the growing mountain of sins
I'm committing this morning.

Until Then

~ for Danna Primm
Wednesday, January 27

Growing up, it was… Just you wait until
your father gets home, or the Lord
comes again… or worse…
wait until marriage.

For my dad,
growing up in Oklahoma,
it was… until the cows come home.

With my daughter, for 20 years,
it was an eternity of… wait
till you're old enough
to understand.

The last 21 years,
for me, have been…
until that next book hits
my doorstep in a few boxes
of 30 or more, so I can smell
the end of my sweat and means.

For some of the darker days,
it has been… waiting until
test results come back.

For the Jews it has long been…
L'Shana Haba'ah B'Yerushalayim,
until "Next year in Jerusalem!"
at the end of Passover,
or on Yom Kippur.

For four years now,
it has been… until
the White House
has new tenants.

For the last six months,
it has been… waiting until
mom and dad finally receive
the vaccine.
          Now, it is until
they get the second dose,
and I get the first.

ALL IT TOOK

~ for Norma Brown
Thursday, January 28

Somewhere, in the year of 1937,
they noticed she was drawing
a lot, by the age of five…
and she began painting
in the fourth grade,
because her dad,
the principal,
offered to pay
their art teacher
to stay after school
and give her lessons.

By high school, she was
selling some of her works,
which is why, down the road,
as a mother of three in the 1970s,
she stood, gape-jawed, on a sidewalk
outside Kaune's Neighborhood Market,
just across from the gas station there
on Old Santa Fe Trail, when she
caught site of a woman filling
her car at one of the pumps
and soon realized it was
Georgia O'Keeffe.

She never recovered.

At 88, she still speaks
of the moment in soft
and very reverent tones.

And I'm guessing it's why,
after I graduated years later...

she picked up the brushes again...
and has never stopped painting since.

WHAT POETS NEED TO KNOW
ABOUT ROAD SIGNS

~ for Patrick Marshall
Friday, January 29

The white ones with black letters
are trying to tell you what you
should, or shouldn't, do…
for instance, you're going
too fast here in this line,
or too slow in that stanza.
Or… maybe you shouldn't
park that piece of crap there.

The yellow ones serve as viable
warnings about what lies ahead…
among your favorites… to ignore…
unless one has to do with soft shoulders,
then you're all eyes and hopes for it to be so.

(Since running head-on into hazards
is one of the patterns of your life
that led you to this profession.)

Green ones intend to guide.
They want you to know where
you are or, with big white arrows,
which way you might want to go…

as well as the number of miles
to your imagined destination?

Blue ones avail you of helpful
services: hospitals or editors;
gas stations or workshops;
lodging, because you've
been at it far too long;
or rest areas, because
you forget to breathe.

The orange ones let you know
that there is necessary maintenance
taking place up ahead. So slow down
and consider it for the metaphor it is.

And, finally, that octagonal red one?
Look… if you still have to be told?
I'm afraid little else can be done.

THANKS ANYWAY

~ for a fairly well-known author who offered
to write a blurb for the next book
Saturday, January 30

You thanked me for sharing
the sample of my poems...
as if you were my brother.

You liked a couple even.
Particularly the one on
sourdough I included.
But then you said that
you simply must admit,
you are "not much into
directly political poems."

You could understand
the release in writing
such stuff, but even
an Adrienne Rich
couldn't make it
work for long.

Then, without
a paragraph break...
you launched into being
"from the South (if Texas

is the South)," and capitalized
the "S" both times, which remains
the political spelling of that regionally
derogatory term, at least for those who
move to the Northeast and make a big
point of doing so, for political reasons.

So, I of course wrote out a response
that I of course did not send to you.

Dear Such 'n' Such,

I too dislike political poetry.
Unfortunately, it's been a critical
part of the poet's job description for
thousands of years. *The Iliad* was a work
of military and political propaganda, back
around the time of Moses and Troy, et al.

Also, Dante's *Inferno* was an outright act
of political indignance. Ovid? Or Pablo
Neruda? booted from their beloved
countries. But surely politics had
nothing to do with it. Dante,
if you recall, was so exiled,
his sons were not allowed
to ever return to Florence.

Alas, most people must
deal with certain aspects
of a job they don't enjoy,
for instance book signings
at bookstores that nobody
shows up to... maybe you
have experienced that too?

Anyway, I want to thank you
for your anemic consideration.
And though a rather shameless
act of self-promotion at the end
sounded sincere—an invitation
to check out your latest reboot
of an outdated book with a title
so classist, racist, and, political?
that I refuse to repeat it here...
as it refers to the hard-edged
people I grew up around—

I am afraid I am too busy
to give it the attention
it might deserve.

OUT WHERE

Sunday, January 31

Traveling through
the state of West Texas—
which is as different from the state
of East Texas as Arizona is from
Mississippi… or, Alabama—
you'll see some of the things
God left undone on Earth,
which is an art of its own.

In the Lower Panhandle,
you'll also see a far horizon
as level as the Pacific Ocean.

There aren't a lot of beholders
out in these boundless expanses,
but among the ol'-timers you will
find those who see the beauty in it.

For me it's always been the romance
of places where rotting fence posts
outnumber humans 10,000 to 1,

where a coyote's free to roam,
or to be kicked by a donkey

if it gets too close to
other kin on the farm,

where a rattlesnake takes
to the rare retreats of shade
when the sun sinks fiery teeth
into the hours of an afternoon,

and where I'm eternally reminded
of the magnitude of what's been lost
to the insatiable machine of progress.

February ... ...

We are two tumbleweeds hurrying
through the universe.

~ Robert Bly

PALO DURO CANYON

To hike inside
the second largest canyon
the U. S. has to offer, requires
a regular reminder that one is not
scaling anything... those red ridges
towering above each shoulder are
the crust that forms the surface
of the Southern Great Plains.

This is not a mountain range
blocking the way out west
to that Golden Coastline.
This isn't from the thrust
of restless tectonic plates.

This is the Earth opening
herself up to allow pilgrims
into her lower realms—ones
she normally keeps hidden—
lips pried apart by the ancient
tempers of the wind and water.
This is one of a million reasons
we know the Earth is a mother.

PARTING THE WATERS

Tuesday, February 2

The confluence of the Palo Duro
and the Tierra Blanca creeks forms
the main tributary to the Red River,
the menstrual stream that constitutes
the great geographical and mythological
scar that runs down the length of my life,
having been born out in the piney woods
of East Texas, but raised, and educated,
in the heart and hubcap of Oklahoma,
before moving back across, over 40
years later, to the Texas Hills outside
Austin—where the hate for that state
above burns the hottest and brightest.
Not even Moses, with the aid of God
and his rod, could part that dark mud.
But to know now how the headwaters
of my own personal River Styx took
some ninety million years to carve out
this magnificent canyon... long before
humans began to give unavailing names
to all their tribal and petty divisions...
I am blessed to learn... even if late
in the game... that I was borne of
a paleolithic patience and beauty.

FIVE WAYS TO LEAVE

Wednesday, February 3

The sky above these ridges
is bodacious, as much as blue.
But, take your eye off the ground
for long and you'll soon be the prey
of broken stones twisting an ankle,
if not both, to bring you down to
the razory edge of their level.

And in the falling, you may well
meet with the sabertoothed needles
of a prickly pear cactus going purple
in the blister of a February's wind.
Needles that will leave memories
when you try to pull them out.

And in the dodging of those,
watch out for the knife blades
of the yucca, or the spear-head
thorns of a cranky mesquite tree.

But, all said, the best way to decrease
your odds of survival would be between
the curvaceous and quite capable fangs
of a rattlesnake, if she rings her bell
one or two seconds… too late.

They Have Their Reasons

~ for Catherine Lanham,
Jason Mote, and Larry Martin
Thursday, February 4

A friend who knows
says "the landscape is
an acquired taste." Yes,
the canyons are beautiful,
but most of the western half
of the panhandle is a tabletop,
the Caprock, this sandpapered
plateau cut so flat you could tile
most of it. She went on to tell me
"that said, the sheer preponderance
of sky is gorgeous. The simplicity
of land… horizon… sky
grows on a person."

I quoted her because
she is a poet… even if
nonpracticing… for now.

The people here, she said less
about, because she is gracious…
reads books, and still believes that
climate change is real, and that Jesus
might have had a "socialism problem."

A very different friend, from years back,
one of the few I have known who was
a better cynic than I, grew up here,
in The Town Without a Frown,
Happy, Texas, just a few miles
south of the canyon, and all
he ever said about it was
"It was far from it."

One other friend
who went to college
in Canyon, when it was
West Texas State, told me,
because I had asked him why,
    hey n. it was the only school with
    a good art program that offered
    me a football scholarship…

And I quoted him because
that is just an unbelievable
and awesome thing for him,
or anyone, to say. Am I right?

Anyway, if I ever make another
friend, I'll tell you their story too.

THE SILENCE THAT COULD

~ for Andrea & John Byers
Friday, February 5

There is a hideout
built of hard wood
and stone that holds
to the scar-ridden skin
and bone of the Caprock
near the rim of the canyon.

It stands firm, and knee-deep
in mesquite and sparse patches
of buffalo grass… a barrel chest
braced against the relentless wind.

And though I've never made friends
or family very well, it comes with both.
Horses, a donkey, even a Shetland pony.
Two cats and Diego, a wild-eyed tiny goat.
All of us rescued from our previous lives.

But in the evenings, if the wind grants
a reprieve, there is a wood-slat swing
on a screened-in porch.
                    And with it
comes a dusky silence in the purple
dimming air. A silence I too often

forget still exists. A silence
attached to the bone
of the Caprock.

A silence that
could save a race
from the ignorance
of unremitting noise...

if we would simply give it
the time, and the invitation.

HOODOOS AND SLOTS

Each time I encounter
yet another glorious work
of interstellar art for the first
time and behold wonders like
slot canyons and red hoodoos
formed of sandstone and shale,

I want it to reach out and hug me,
maybe pet my head, and tell me
it will be fine. And it will still
be here, long after humans'
ingenuity for self-destruction
has self-fulfilled that prophecy.

Which of course renews my desire
to encourage humans to stop
all that destruction
and fulfilling.

Which of course
could possibly occur
if humans would turn off
all of our little mind-numbing
inventions and sit for long periods

in the silence and shadows of glories
like red hoodoos and slot canyons
formed of shale and sandstone.

Which of course is a thing
I've mentioned, a gentle
suggestion I have made,
a thousand times or more,

and will continue making,
you know, just to bug you.

THE CENTER THAT HOLDS

~ for Jill Douglas
Sunday, February 7

There is a line,
a cord thin and frayed
by the hard tugging of surprises
and trials in life, that holds nonetheless,
as it runs down the steep mountain
of generations, from a mother
to a mother, to daughters,
sons, grandsons and on.

It is the strong heart
that passes through
all the rings of a tree
on its way to the roots
that sustain a good family.

It is the cleft, between crags,
collecting rain into a little creek
that carves its way through stone
over the lifetimes it takes to make
the river we call our own. And even
in the rough seasons when the bed
runs dry, it still remains the path
that will faithfully lead us
down to that great sea.

WHAT WE NEED

~ for Stephanie Gibson
Monday, February 8

It's not news
to say love is blind.
Like shouting "Eureka!"
at bread in the grocery store.

But keep in mind that love is also
deaf, and can't smell very well either.
You'll be grateful when he's a teenager
with a drum set who stuffs his socks
under the pillow to make it look
like he's "cleaned his room."

For now though, stare
into his sleeping face
every chance you get.
You will miss that one,
when he locks his door,
or leaves home for college.

And when you worry about
the world that he'll someday
walk in, do try to remember
how desperately that world
needs a son whose mother

thinks, reads books, loves art,
and takes him to the Met,
or the "latest, greatest"
thing on Broadway,
even if he acts like
he doesn't want to.

Because, that stuff
sinks in. And, that is
the stuff he will use to
give this madmad world
its best chance to keep on.

In the meantime… buck up,
and eat well. Parenting is not
for the weak of sleep, which
you already know.
                    That's just
something an already-parent
says who lay awake all night
worrying about his daughter
who's camping in a canyon
somewhere in Oklahoma
with an older boyfriend
who "seems" nice, but
because he is a boy,

and you were one,
you don't trust him,

which is why we need
better mothers to raise
better boys.
         Like I said,
it's really our only chance.

WE'VE GOT THIS

~ for Andrew Pastides
Monday, February 8

It's best to ignore the role
of just about every father
in the recurring plot line
of just about every play
from Shakespeare to
Arthur Miller and on…

and remember that you do
matter.
          Fathers can be good.

(Maybe yours was an example.
I know, for sure, that mine was.)

Every time he rolls his eyes and sighs
in embarrassment at one of your jokes,
know that he'll miss it when you're gone,

and that a man of great passions for art
and good tastes in Mezcal and baklava
is being observed all along the way…

as it took over 20 years for my Sierra

to drop her right hand from her hip
and finally find the words to tell me.

The soul of a man is the biggest of all
hand-me-downs. That's why I blame
fathers for the sons who blaspheme
beauty in a wake of supreme hate.

It's why, every day, the rest of us
must take yet another deep breath
and strive, once again, to do better.

AND THEN, THE NEXT

~ for Beth Honeycutt
Tuesday, February 9

I inherited it from my mother,
a talent for forgetting to breathe,
the ability to shut down my body's
bio-reflexes in order to thoroughly
worry about something, or other.

Of course the lungs eventually
cry out for the exchange of
carbon dioxide with that
superior gas… oxygen.
But, I've been known
to push the system's
operational limits.

Add to this gift
a pandemic, and…
oh God, have mercy,
it just happened again…

that's why I now set aside
times throughout every day
to wander among the stones
I have stacked as monuments
to the sheer mass and volume

of all that one *can* let go,
if one is willing to strive.

And in those thousands
upon thousands I have
picked up, brushed off,
contemplated, and placed,

each one of them represents

a breath

I remembered to take.

In, Out, Repeat

~ for Beth Honeycutt
Wednesday, February 10

I have taken to double-masking.
It's personal, as much as medical.
I love the added protection against
the exhalations of those in the aisles
at the grocery store who wear t-shirts
that have 'Jesus Saves' stenciled over
American flags and crossed AK-47s.

That said, I am also twice as aware
of this year's disruption of breath,
the breathing I took for granted,
and thus forgot to do at times,
in the plain air of 'life before.'

I'm getting to know my lungs
again, if not for the first time.
I appreciate, so much more,
what they have been up to
all my life, and I do hope
they'll continue to do it.

As a bonus, the masks
remind me how crucial
it is to brush my teeth…

at least twice a day. Or…
maybe before every outing.

I have two good friends who
are deeply reconnected to their
breath, and the art of breathing,
because of how painful it is to do.
They're reminded every few seconds.

And what they might say to us is…

Take advantage. Draw that stuff
down in as far as the diaphragm
can pull it. Feel the miracle it is.
Take it outside today on a walk.

Love it, warm, cold or burning,
because there is, ultimately,
a limited supply.

On Cures and Causes

~ for Terry Clark
Thursday, February 11

Phase 4 in the chart
of vaccine distribution
from the CDC and NIH
reads, without the least
bit of humor intended,

    "Everyone residing
    in the United States
    who did not have
    access to the vaccine
    in previous phases."

As a male in his mid-50s,
currently sort of employed
as poet-for-hire, who's taken
decent care of every organ,
except maybe his liver,
I hope I'm still alive
when they finally call
for the end of the line.

So, to the young woman
growing cultures in a lab
at 3:00 a.m. and filling up

small bottles of the good stuff
on bottomless cups of lukewarm
coffee in a fluorescent breakroom,
know that I am rooting you on…
during the hours I am awake.

Oh, and by the way…
could you make sure
your little concoction
also takes on the other
mutant ninja variations?

With that too much in mind,
should the day arrive, that day
when I qualify, sometime around
the middle of the summer in 2022,
I will then have to hope I survive
the side-effects of a second dose.
I've been hearing mixed reports.

Years ago, my best friend died
of a damn cure they gave him.
Which has me contemplating
that ambiguous, unsettling
specter of root causes.

In Our Own Image

It's the god we have made of God
that has tossed our salvation
onto the chopping block
and raised its mighty
cleaver up high.

The one that vows
to destroy, by way of
his 30-round magazines,
the enemies we've created.

The one that continues to insist,
by chapter and verse, that a slave
should fluff the masters' pillows,
bring out his big bowl of gumbo,
and be happy to have a damn job.

The one that loves thy neighbor,
unless thy neighbor wears her
hijab, or burns a menorah
every year at Hanukkah.

Or the one that polishes up
the climax in his sermon notes

in a cheap motel room somewhere
on the backstreets of Baton Rouge,
while he waits for a male prostitute.

This god we have made of God
has now set his new XPS2
Holographic Weapon
Sights on God
himself…

and his right
index finger
is twitching.

THE TIME WE HAVE

~ for Jymmie Stanton
Saturday, February 13

There is time.
And all the time
there's too much…
and too little… of it.

And, after living a good
long time, there's more than
enough of it to reflect, on what
was good—the beauties, the loves,
the blaze of maple leaves in October,
that first kiss, that did us in altogether.
Yet maybe there's not enough to fret
over the times we got it all wrong
and backwards… those dumb
things we said to our kids,
the worse things we did.

And, there will always be
enough time to hope—hope
that most of it can be forgiven,
much of it maybe even forgotten.
Question is… will we have enough
for there to be some amount of
hope for coming generations

(the kids of those kids that
we said dumb things to)
to say and do better...
when it comes to the hot
mess of a globe... this ball...
we played a little too hard with.

Which isn't funny when we consider
how we have always made time to plan
for life's big disasters and contingencies,
with health, home, and car insurance—
even the death insurance we call life.
But how seldom we set aside time
to plan for the remote possibility
that ol' Samwise Gamgee may
have been onto something...
when he turned to Gandalf
and queried, "Is everything
sad going to come untrue?"

Which suggests, maybe
we should take more
if not most of what
time we have left

         to play?

HIS FOOTSTEPS

~ for G.K. (Kim) Stanton
Sunday, February 14

Dad was a good pastor…
teacher instead of preacher,
listener as much as talker…
a model they used to make
back before the big screens,
a house band, fog machines,
and the laser-light freak shows
of Joel Osteen or Jesse Duplantis
in private jets, or Lamborghinis—
Satan's own black operations team.

In other words, that sound outdated,
my father is a humble and decent man.

And though I struggle with those qualities,
often judged an odd sheep out of the flock,
not everyone knows I am, or at least was,
a licensed minister in my home state.

I doubt I'd pass inspection now.
My blinkers are out, the taillights
don't work, and I certainly have
no headlamps to get me back,
where I hope they'd have me.

But I carry the old set of tools
that he handed down to me.

With poetry as my pulpit,
he taught me to never
step up behind it
unprepared…
or as a bully.

With the open
road as my altar,
and great cathedral,
he taught me that God
has never needed walls, nor
denominations, to hide behind.

And, with all creation… its beauty,
its hope, and its need for salvation…
as my fervent message, he taught me
that three points, three illustrations,
are about as much as an average
churchgoer can stomach.

AMONG THE ELEMENTS

~ for Danna Primm
Monday, February 15

As long as I have water
to boil and the grounds
to slowly pour it over,
I will continue to get
under the earth's skin
with the cut of paper
and blood of a pen.

And, if the world
runs out of paper,
or ink for the pens,
then I'll draw poems
with a left forefinger
in the scorch of sand.

*   *   *

As long as I have earth
to spread with seeds…
and then to walk among
their fruits and forests…
ancient stones to gather,
or rest beside, and soak in
their long, steady vibrations,

a subsonic song of the eons,
I will hum along with it all
my anthems to the glories
of the dirt and the trees,
the rocks and the leaves.

*　　*　　*

And, as long as I have fire
to burn those poems back into
the ashes from whence they came,
among the flames of The Muses
and their blistering inspiration,

I'll know that I have a place…
that I do serve my purpose…

among the myriad miracles
that fill the air we breathe.

A Cup of Coffee

~ for Karen Zundel
Tuesday, February 16

Woke up to a negative-something
wind-chill factor and no water.
Still have electricity, but…
we have been warned.

So, there's a stack
of wood just inside
the front door. And,
there are jars, clay jugs,
pitchers, and liquor bottles
littering the dining room table,
even big pots on the unlit stove,
all full of water—enough for most
things, except maybe flushing toilets.

It's gonna be a frigid day in the woods for me…
I muse, standing amidst the jars and pots.
Which has me thinking more than usual
about the cup of coffee I will make…
damn the consequences… because
that cup is the pilot of this ship.

Every poem in this, or every
other book, was discovered

by Columbia—and that dark
brood of all beans on deck—
standing steadfast at that helm.

So my teeth may not get brushed
this morning... but a tequila rinse
should do the trick. And, as I said,
the cedar trees, two empty lots over,
may have to serve as today's porcelain
cathedral. And I will be nothing to smell,
or look at, by the time evening rolls around.

But at least one, good, cup of coffee
is, as you may be sensing,
nonnegotiable.

One, Two, Fourth, or Fifth

~ for Danna Primm and Karen Zundel
Wednesday, February 17

So, one day of no water
runs into two; for some,
a day without electricity
now turns into a fourth,
or fifth… and the lamp
I write by just flickered,
again.
    The blackest gray sky
rained ice through the night,
tapping out some dated code
of long and short signals…
an alphabet almost no one
remembers—since Martin
Cooper invented that weird
looking handheld cell phone.

This morning, that lost code
drips from the tips of arctic
silver daggers, into buckets
I've set out there, in hopes
of flushing the two toilets.

And here I am thinking,
again, on a second day:

As long as I have water
to boil and the grounds
to slowly pour it over,

I am going to make
that one cup of coffee,
damn the consequences,

because that one good cup
is still...
                nonnegotiable.

LINEAGE

~ for John Roche
Thursday, February 18

Reading: the birth mother
of resistance, the sire bond
of rebellions and revolutions
when the world goes mad for
the Attilas, Bloody Marys, and
the Khans and Vladimirs about.

And in these drawn-out months
of barely this, not enough that,
and when the hell will it end...

the poets who held on before me
are the foundation of my resilience.

Jeffers commands me to serve it up,
even when it's hard, or depressing.

Baudelaire reminds me there is
at least one angel hovering
above every darkness.

Dante proves that hell
is not forever, as long as
you watch your mouth, and

just keep walking… don't stop.

Bukowski seems to say I will find
a sideways joy within the madness,
if I believe that I was born into this.

Stephen Dunn, my Obi-Wan Kenobi,
teaches me what it means to *be* a Jedi,
and not just play one on television…
who personally patted me on my back
to silently assure the force is with me.

Pablo Neruda insists it comes down
to the salt air of the Pacific and love.

Tony Mares, a mentor and friend, he
reminds me there is always one more
wound. But that, it too, will be okay.

Sharon Olds dares me. Zagajewski
is my brother in this sweet sadness.
Hoagland ordains my snarky punk.

And Rumi bids me to come and sit
at the long table of companionship.
It is time for all of us to drink, and
laugh at this whole damn business.

DEAR JANE

~ for John Roche
Friday, February 19

She's holding Walter,
my grandpa's uncle,
on her lap, in a copy
of a copy of a printed
.jpeg downloaded from
Ancestry.com by my dad's
niece's husband, who I am told
is police chief in Duncan, Oklahoma.

She married Francis Marion Brown,
and they had two sons, Walter and
Levi Lee, my great-grandfather,
known as "Lefty." Could be
where I got that from?

Anyway, Lefty married
Arizona Reynolds, before
he married Nora Simmons.

And I don't know yet if it was
Nora or Arizona who gave birth
to my grandpa, Vernie Brown, but,
I love the sound of Lefty and Arizona.

And as I look at what I guess is
a tintype photograph of my great-
great-grandmother, with taut, dark
skin, searing obsidian eyes, and heavy
mane of black hair thick and long enough
to catch a baby falling from the firmament,

I do not need Ancestry.com to tell me
this woman fully bled Cherokee…
though… it does nonetheless.

Her name was Jane Wren…
before the Brown was added.

And, I suddenly feel more solid.
Solid as the red earth of my home.

AT LEAST TWICE

~ for John Roche
Saturday, February 20

> Our parents died at least twice,
> the second time when we forgot
>   their stories,
>
> ~ Stephen Dunn

When the lines go down,
no electricity runs
to the past.
Rooms go dark…
and the stories that lived
in them flee into the moonlight.
Now, only a good hunter, the best
of trackers with the nose of a hound,
has any chance of picking up the trail.
If we don't know the ilk we come from,
who in the hell do we plan on being?
Even Adam and Eve had theirs…
a story made from dirt, and a rib.
And if we lose that one, all we have
left is the next episode of *The Batchelor*
for the coming generations—generations
that will be at least twice as lost as ours,
with no home worth returning to.

WHERE WE AGREE

The coyote and I do not agree
on what is tasty—what's worth
yipping about to the half moon.

But, we do agree that the world
is full of delicious things to eat,
if we are patient… and aware.

We do not agree on timing,
prep, cooking procedures,
or how to present a table.

But, we do agree a stuffed
belly is enough, that to kill
more is a waste of resource.

We don't agree on the hours
to keep, the length of shifts,
or what to do with time off.

But, we do agree our work
is sufficient for our days…
that tomorrow will come,

or it won't.

FRIENDS ARE FOR

~ for Konrad & Darra Eek,
from Rusty & Lynde Myers
Monday, February 22

The fortune cookie reads:

> You will have many friends
> when you need them.

What it fails to mention is
the condition: As long as
you've been a good one
to others along the way.

The Chinese, historically,
have left quite a bit unsaid,
which we could learn from.

But now that you've come
to the time of your need—

days when poems, prayers,
and promises are more than
an old John Denver song—

your friends arrive, bearing
all three on seasoned wings

of the many years we've traveled
the backroads of this good Earth.

It takes a true heart to be a friend,
the kind of heart that takes in one's
prodigal daughter for an in-between
and necessary time—or walks others
through the midnight of losing a son.

So here we are to return the favors,
because, as one mystic poet bids:

> *The world is full of seasons...*
> *of anguish... of laughter...*

And one equation of love
is... both must be shared.

But as that great northern
prophet, Bruce Cockburn,
sings a bit later in the song,

> *Isn't that what friends are for*
> (then he repeats...
> for good measure)
> *Isn't that what friends are for*

DOWN TO THIS

~ for Lou Kohlman
Tuesday, February 23

In the days after Christmas,
you broke an ankle, as a last
little gift to yourself… there
in the season that keeps on
giving. And you try to laugh
at the stupid joke… but…

it's now February-something,
and you've left the house only
four times since December 27th.

So, what once was just a pandemic,
has now turned into a level of doing
very close to nothing whatsoever that
would test any overactive imagination.

By now thumbs are sore from twiddling,
finger bones are tired of rapping the arm
of the chair, and it is too late to pick up
knitting, or learn how to cross-stitch.

So, you've decided to take a course
in the nature of stillness, patience,
and acceptance. Not all that easy

for a brain that's used to thinking
steps ahead to the next six things,
all having self-imposed deadlines.

But an elevated leg fills long days
with moments—each one asking
to be considered.

            There's a length
to breath, in its coming and going,
that can be followed and explored
without any reason to measure it.

Time is stripped of its uniform...
those rows of medals and badges.

And the thought suffuses your mind,

            There may be... another way.

TILT AND SHIFT

~ for Andrea Byers
Wednesday, February 24

The raised and curved tail
of a quarter moon tickles
the hackles of the dancing
coyotes.
           She hears their hot
laughter as they hunt for more
than just food in the deep night
of a panhandle drought.
                    Enough
light for her to walk the canyon by,
unafraid, she wants to join in with
the happy cries and all that close
heavy breathing it takes to live
thoroughly in the moment…

tomorrow be damned…
all we need is water, love,
and the heave of hormones.

And so… as that manic song
begins to well up from within
the dark temple of her desire,
the first thing she tosses is…
the tyranny of domestication.

Further down the trail, she then
lets go any and every inhibition.

Which is, by some ancient decree,
followed by each piece of clothing.

ONE, MAYBE TWO

~ for the next generation
Thursday, February 25

I will not save the world.
But today I'm going to do
one little thing, maybe two,
to help the firm young minds
who might just pull that off…

like play the acoustic guitar…
instead of the electrified one.

And, I may walk off, away,
into the wooded lots nearby
to do my business. And I may
just do it twice… which would
save about five gallons of water.
I might just make this a habit…
which would save 1,825 a year.

Tonight, I will let this almost full
Snow Moon be my only nightlight.
Which would be three things I did.

And, if I want to get crazy with it,
I will eat yesterday's leftovers cold.
Yes, no RF radiation in this house.

I will also look up every word
in my fat dictionary with pages,
instead of using Siri, who uses
Google and all of its exabytes
and its zettabytes of storage.

Tomorrow, I will take down
some of the Christmas lights
in the front yard that we have
been clinging to for the residue
of joy they leave on the darkness
that 2020 dropped at our doorstep.

And I'll drive a car absolutely nowhere.
Since I haven't had anywhere to be
for going on eleven months now.

And soon… soon, I tell you…

I am going to plant something,
like a flower… or maybe a tree.

WHAT A WASTE

Left to my own poor judgment,
I wasted a perfectly good day…
while Ashley was working away
on things that pay electric bills.

And yet, knowing her the way
I do, I am certain that a certain
amount of play was also a part
of her more productive day…

not that mine wasn't productive.
As you can see, I had some time
to play around myself with a bit
of poor, and haphazard, rhyme.

But, I'm bored with all that now.
This is about my perfectly wasted
day, and how I spent much of it
wandering around under clouds,

building a fire, despite the mist,
digging stones out of damp dirt
and then listening for the song,
the singing space to place one.

The spot among thousands
where it will take its rightful
throne in the mad cause of art.
Math is beauty... beauty is math.

Physics is poetry... more like it.
And it's for the sake of poetry,
Mary Oliver's to be specific,
that I did this with my one

wild and precious day today.
And I believe, having done it,
that this was time well wasted...
and that I should waste more of it.

FRONT AND CENTER

~ for Terri Stubblefield
Saturday, February 27

Let me sing another song
up to the front lines today.

To a pastor in Connecticut
who's reaching out to touch
the quivering hand—through
latex gloves—of a parishioner,
who had to watch a daughter die
behind glass, in a tangle of tubes,
to offer no prayer through a mask,
since no prayer would do. Not now.

To the nurse up in Minneapolis, who
had Covid herself, and felt the death
in its grip, but who now has to turn
to a family outside a window, down
on the sidewalk, to signal with eyes
that the end has come, and is gone.

To a doctor in North Carolina who
never thought, as the acting chief
of surgery, that she would long
for the days of broken bones
and knee replacements.

To a first responder who
bursts into dangerous air
every time a call comes in.

To a caregiver whose mind
is not allowed any days off,
who counts pills in her sleep,
worries if she cleaned the mail
and cans of soup from the store
enough to be safe, and wonders if,
when her time comes, she'll receive
the same kindness and consideration.

To a mental health worker in Austin
who is applying a tourniquet, best
he can, to the collective psyche
of a species, but knows the sheer
level of loss that's already occurred
will alter the shape of a generation.

We do not know all that you are
going through, but we do have
an idea where we wouldn't be
without the work you've done.

THE END IS NOT NEAR ENOUGH

Sunday, February 28

This, the last day of February
in the year 2021, symbolically
marks the first anniversary of
that gathering of wicked clouds
on a fading horizon of normalcy.

Evening news anchors no longer
had to fake their terrible concern.
China could no longer contain all
the evidence piling up on the curb.
And people were getting on planes.

I was packing books and wrapping up
a People's Poetry Festival in the salt air
of Corpus Christi, about to strike out
on the road again—a delicate career
I was beginning to worry might soon
be teetering yet again on nonexistence.

But, I've worried about that plausibility
on a monthly basis for a good 20 years.

Still, the general mess of the world felt
a little messier than usual. People were
dying in large numbers, and it was not

from the deranged minds of Caesars
and Pol Pots, or the Benito Mussolinis
this time, despots who never disappear,
but, forever come again in the creepy
form of failed New York real estate
mongrels, or some such grossness.

No… now it was at the microscopic
hands of a clever bug, one quite gifted
at procreation, and tireless adaptability.

And here, a year later, the news remains
just as confusing, just as noncommittal
in its interpretations of the data… and,
therefore, the same amount of useless.

March ... ...

... to know that one life
    has breathed easier
because you lived here.
This is to have succeeded.

~ Ralph Waldo Emerson

PATRONS AND SAINTS

~ for those who host
Monday, March 1

I doubt I was ever a convenience.
So, thank God for making kind souls
who too often use poor judgment when
it comes to carrying out their kindness.

You took in, and offered some sheets,
a pillow, and more important, a room
with a bath, a sink… and that other
absolute necessity… to a traveler,

this wandering bard who can't
make his living on motel rooms
with forgotten germs, and always
one long hair in a dripping shower,

a secret creed among housekeepers
they will not appreciate me sharing.
They have others… but this poem
is about you and your generosity.

I've had the undeserved fortune
of planked salmon and asparagus
seared on a smoky grill, and served
on deck with a mad view of Olympia

and the boats afloat in Budd Inlet.
I have sipped Don Abraham tequila
with a rock-star chef, who lives within
strolling distance of Long Island Sound.

I've shared an evening of poems and songs,
laughing tears and margaritas, in a packed
house during sunset on Boca Ciega Bay
in a nook of St. Petersburg, Florida.

And, I have had the privilege of
undisturbed quiet on the nights
when I have also had too much
human interaction for one week.

You are patrons, saints of the arts.
Many of you I now count as friends.
And if I ever lose the Pulitzer Prize…
you will all be invited to the afterparty.

Raging Silence

~ for the voiceless
Tuesday, March 2

For the seven-year-old boy
sitting in a closet, lights off,
casting about for magic spells,
Invisibility… Disillusionment…
mouthing the soundless syllables:
expecto patronum, expecto patronum…
who cries when he hears the tires
turn into the gravel driveway…

For the eight-year-old girl
clinging to a pink backpack,
frozen, wondering where all of
the empty diamonds of chain-link
came from that are surrounding her,
grasping for words in a weird language
she vaguely recognizes from television…

For the elephant, foraging through
the streets of a city in the darkest
middle of some African night,
craving that pulp and juice
of mangos along the musky
ancestral trail humans ignored
when they kept building homes…

For the sad-eyed shaggy
abandoned little mutt-pup,
lying, solid as a cedar stump,
in her cage at the rescue center,
believing, if she stays still enough,
no one will happen to notice her…
the only defense she's ever known…

Know that your eyes are handing over
the most important story, and some
of us are hanging on every word
that you are not able to say…

HEAD-SCRATCHER

~ for Texas Governor Greg Abbott
Wednesday, March 3

We met at the sesquicentennial
celebration of our hometown,
Longview. Well, we did not
meet. We, more so, passed
like two VIPs in the night
at a party that had maybe
invited a few too many?

You… a governor… I…
a poet. We had no reason
to stop and chat. Agreed?

And since I had no chance
to ask, I'll assume that you
are, or were, a decent man—
that you entered this business
for something like the good of
the people of our unwieldy state.

Which leads to my next question.

What happens?

What is it that inevitably flips

the good-sense-that-God-
gave-a-goldfish switch
in most politicians?

I'll await your answer.

As I am still awaiting some
reply from Oklahoma's version
of you... who also happens to be
from my hometown (I have two)...
because I wrote him a poem as well.

His might have sailed over his brow,
though, I'm afraid. That's why I kept
this simple, and straight to the point.

FOR THE NIGHT

~ for Riha Rothberg
Thursday, March 4

The horizon is an obsidian tree line,
a serrated blade slicing into twilight
for the juice of a long-waning day.

The clouds are a murder of crows,
plumes of dark and gnarled fingers
pulling back what's left of the sky.

But in between them, just enough
of a glow to guide us homeward,
an incandescence that serves as

a promise for the sun's due
return, and the eventual
warmth of tomorrow.

START SOMEWHERE

~ for Harold Covington,
leader of the Northwest Front
Friday, March 5

If I could have you chained
to a chair, the mouth gagged,
in some undisclosed location…

it would only make matters worse,
and reinforce the ramparts you stalk,
spark growth in the tumor of your hate.

But while I have you there, I would still
like to say, your dreams are not national,
to reinvent a wheel you believe is square,

to take Washington, Oregon, Idaho, and
western Montana, and create some Israel
free of Jews, and every measurable shade

of each kind of color known to our species.
No, that's just your attention-grabbing ruse.
What you want is to defeat a terrible sense

of loneliness, a strange new form of it,
brought into being by overpopulation.
You fear erasure *before* the Apocalypse.

You're afraid of demotion, becoming lost,
or worse, insignificant, in the human crowd,
after barbarously running the show for eons.

And what this has to do with your mother,
or father, we'll not have time to go into.
But we both know it's in the big mix.

I just want you to take this time,
as we are deciding what to do
with the raging likes of you,

to reflect on what forced
the likes of us to need
to have this little talk.

COME ON HOME

~ for Dr. Tim Zeddies
Sunday, March 7

If you threw your baby out
with the bathwater so long ago
you don't remember when now...
one of the best things you could do
for that self is to take some time
out of every day from here on
to re-get to know it better.

The television's not
your friend, and...
that little smartphone
is only pretending to be...
to get into your head and wallet.
We actually forget it has an off switch.

When my first marriage ended, I felt
terrible that I didn't feel worse...
that I wasn't more desolated
and lonely.

Thing was...
I just invited myself
to come on home
and live with me.

We'd been so close,
years before, we easily
took up where we left off.

But, as happens, I lost it again…
somehow, somewhere, somewhen,

and so, here in the days of waiting…
waiting for some vaccine… waiting
for governors to screw their heads
back on… waiting for my career
to return…

I'm feeling a need.

WE EVEN SHARE A MIDDLE NAME

~ for Mason Lee Zundel
Monday, March 8

It begins in middle school…
we start to notice that half, or
more, of the other boys wiping
their noses and talking nonstop
in the stinky halls are so stupid,
we kind of feel embarrassed for
their sisters, mothers, and fathers.

Though a sensitive soul, like you are,
and I was, would never say anything.
So, we go quiet, and begin thinking
too much about things we'd simply
wondered about in the years before.

We realize that our passions are not
necessarily shared by those jerks…

and so we keep our interests close,
like the journaling and genealogy…
or grandmothers and gravestones…

but especially the books and movies,
like, say, *Tarzan of the Apes* for me…
or Marty in *Back to the Future* for you.

Usually one, sometimes two, teachers
along the way spot what's going on
and give us the wink we'll be fine.
I hope you have yours. I had mine.

I waited until after I had graduated
to start talking again—no kidding.
You don't need to go for that long.

Just keep this in mind, when you can:
those ancestors, whether above ground
in houses across town, or even resting
beneath markers in the cemetery…

those are the solid shoulders
that you will stand upon
when you come out
the other side.

WHO YOUR FRIENDS ARE

~ for Mia Marie Zundel
Tuesday, March 9

You may have figured out already,
because girls your age are smart,
that girls your age are smarter
than most of the boys your age.

And by the way, science agrees.
But I have found, as an old boy,
though I don't know the science,
that girls stay way smarter forever.

That's why a girl tends to find better
friends, earlier and ever on, much like
the friends you've got in Charlee, a dog,
your cat, Lilo, even Mocha, the hamster.

My wife, who is way older than you are,
still prefers dogs and cats, but especially
horses, to me. So, I have to be careful—
because she's a lot smarter than I am too.

Anyway, you're also likely figuring out
that girls your age, because they are
getting smarter, can, at the same time,
start to make trickier and trickier friends.

So remember, if the going gets rough, your grandmother, just like Charlee, Lilo, even Mocha, she'll be there for you. As good as friends get.

The Way Forward

~ for Audrey Streetman
Wednesday, March 10

My resolve wanes some days,
some more than others…
but the goal remains:

        the ultimate way
to survive a year like this one
would be to stare into its stern
eyes, stand silent in the moonless
midnight of its growing graveyard…
and make resolute peace with mortality.

Then, let the year go, release it back
to the cave that gave birth to it—
watch its silhouette fly on home
in the barely light of predawn.

There is no reasoning with
almost three million bodies
that lived among us last year.

And how many millions does that
leave behind to clean up the messes
those losses have made of our minds?

We'll need that peace treaty we forge
with our final bane… and the truce
we perpetually renew with fear
and all of its rotting fruits
that litter the ground
around our feet.

The only way
we'll ever be able
to get on with the life
that is left for us to live.

CONVERSATION WITH A COUSIN AT A
FAMILY REUNION THAT MAY OR MAY
NOT HAVE TAKEN PLACE

~ for Everett Wilson
Thursday, March 11

Helluva game last Saturday.

    Yup.

Man, that #93 on defense
messed with their QB
for all four quarters.

    Yup. McCoy.

Yeah, that's him. That's the one.

    Gerald McCoy.
    I have him in one
    of my morning classes.

You sit next to him?

    He's a student.
    I'm the teacher.

Seriously?

Yup.

(The cousin rips into a spare rib
and leaves a little sauce on his chin.)

Why's he in your class?

    He's a Human Relations major.
    He has to pass my class
    to play football.

Seriously?

    Yup.

So, he sits behind one o' 'em little desks?

    Well, he sorta engulfs it, more like.

Ha! Yeah, I bet he does.

    He's a big guy.

Hell yeah, he is.

(Another bite.
More sauce.)

So, what's he like?

    One of the nicest students
    I've ever had, actually.

Seriously?

    Yup.

Wha'du'ya know.

    Yeah, and last week,
    as part of a presentation,
    he helped out this one girl by
    coming to the front of the room
    and doing yoga with her…

He did what?

WHAT DO YOU EXPECT?

~ for Everett Wilson
Friday, March 12

My kin come from dust and dirt,
and the harsh Oklahoma wind
that God breathed into them.

And the dirt is as blood-red
as the wind is relentless…

so the garden they imagine
Adam and Eve were given,
is a bit different from yours.

Here, the fruit trees are filled
with as many ants as they are
peaches or pears… and beasts
are family, up to the inevitable
moment when they are eaten.

Out on these southern plains
there's an enormous amount
of room to work with. But…

they manage to work enough
of it to have very little room
leftover for things like irony.

So, when it comes to the slick
speech, sharp suits, shellacked
hair, and the smarmy-ass grins
of those coastal commentators
tellin' 'em how things gotta be,

of course they're gonna vote
with the color of their dirt.

FEAR AND LOATHING IN MINNEAPOLIS

~ for Chad Maslowski
Saturday, March 13

Extreme health conditions
of a pre-pandemic variety
already had you doubled-
down on the isolation thing
last fall. You were playing by
all their latest rules that mostly
recommended doing absolutely
not a thing that did not involve
obtaining toilet paper or eggs.

Then, right around the time of
holly and jolly, and all that stuff,
when Johns Hopkins started in on
scaring folks with talk about variants
that were running the old end-around
on the virus we thought we were soon
going to get a grip on, now that we had
voted out the chief executive problem,
you open an early gift from St. Nick,
or one of his court clerks… and…
find a Summons for Jury Duty.

Suddenly Neil Diamond starts
crooning in your reeling mind,

"a very merry, holly holy,
cherry cherry Christmas,"
and so, you cup your ears
against the onslaught of it
and think, "Holy hell-and-
back, how the heck-and-hell
am I going to not catch Covid
in the hours it will take to get
to that 30-second interview,
where they'll send me straight
away, when they see how clearly
I'm not mentally or emotionally up
for this amount of socially negligent
idiocy and total lack of organization?"

And, well… this year blazed on past
the mile marker for absurdity many
months ago, my friend. So, now…

we're all just holdin' on by the thin
flap on the front of our underwear,
since it appears to be the one item
we still don during Zoom meets.

That is why I was glad to hear
back from you on this today.

CHEERS, SOMEDAY

~ for Dorothy Alexander
Monday, March 15

We will share a birthday tomorrow.
Which one… neither needs to tell.
But for now, it remains the boding
Ides of March. A time that, so far,
has worked out better for the two
of us than it did Caesar, bless 'im.

You were a liberal lesbian judge,
and a lawyer for the indigenous
tribes of far western Oklahoma
during the second half of the 20th
century, which says more than future
generations will be able to comprehend.

You are also a publisher of poetry books.
I don't know which profession is more
dangerous, but you've managed to do
both… and lived to joke about it.

You took on my fifth book
after that Chicago press
passed on it, rather
profanely.
          You said,

"Well, give it to me then,
we'll show the sonofabitch."
I don't recall your exact words?
But, that sure does sound like you.
Anyway, we won the damn Oklahoma
Book Award with that one. Which I did
let him know about. Makes me smile. Still.

You've been sober for almost as long as
it has been since I had my first drink.
But you keep the bottle of 12-year
Chivas Regal up on your mantle
for the day the doctor tells you
you've only got a few days...
maybe a week... at most.

So, I wanted to let you know
that I keep a bottle of the same,
in case the occasion comes along.
I've set it here on my writing table
this morning, to help me with this
poem. Don't worry. I drank coffee.
Enclosed is a picture for 86 proof.
Besides, I want to save it, just like
you are doing. Because, I'd hate
for you to have that drink alone.

ANOTHER YEAR, FOR SURE

Tuesday, March 16

I was blowing out three candles
on a birthday cake while American
soldiers were massacring 500 villagers
in My Lai, Vietnam on this day in 1968.

This time last year, I was writing at length,
in journal 106, about how birthdays for me
went downhill after that, in the 70s and 80s.

I was also wondering who this "Dr. Fauci"
guy is who seems to be on every channel
warning us about a virus that had just
arrived… all smiles… at Terminal 4
in John F. Kennedy International.

So you see what I mean about
birthdays and how they tend
to go for me? Like this one,

which I will spend mostly
refreshing all the various
sundry vaccine websites.

For My Birthday

From the fruits of much labored
clicking, I received the gift of, not
one, but two, opportunities to get
the vaccine… here on my birthday.

Moderna, Dose 1, four hours away
in Palestine, Texas, or the 1-dose,
Johnson & Johnson… right here
in our little Wimberley Pharmacy.

Though the choice would be easy
for most stable minds, of course,
I had to complicate it by asking
ten or more people for opinions.

And my, how they had 'em to give.
I had one actual medical doctor say
they were basically equal. That said,
he'd take Moderna, given a choice.

When I asked my therapist, Dr. Z.,
if I should just stay put and go J & J,
I got a one-word text in response: *Yes*
Followed by the two-word text: *Do it*

Did not bother to punctuate. But then,
both my brothers leaned into Moderna,
using big words, like efficacy 'n' such.
Mom wanted it too, because, for her

youngest son, only the closest thing
to 100% would do. And dad agreed.
A smart man. It went on from there.
And, in the end, I ruled in the favor

of the poet in me, who made the wise
observation that, in most cases like this,
involving the culmination of an entire year
of writing, the big deed should be a journey.

YOU CAN'T MAKE THIS STUFF UP

Wednesday, March 17

And so… journey it is.

I pulled into Palestine…
one of those Texas towns
you can't afford to pronounce
any other way than the way they
mispronounce it… on March 17th
with well over an hour to spare
for my 1:30 appointment.

I killed some of the time
poking around downtown,
because that's how I usually
establish my bearings in towns
of this size. And I can tell you…
it was, most definitely, time killed.

I'll not pass any kind of judgment.
Every town has its unique stories.
And, many deserve to be heard.

But, I noticed considerable
weather and time damage
in structures and streets,
and some of the people.

With still more time to kill,
I parked at a grocery store
near the corner pharmacy
I'd come for, and, oddly,
in a fit of organization...

I checked the confirmation
for my long-awaited blind date
as I masked up to go in and shop.

I was going to grab some easy food
for the Airbnb Ashley set me up with
for the night (because I have lost
my chops for driving all day).

But as I scrolled the email,
I did a double, then triple
take... then one more...
at the date listed there:

Thursday, March 18...

        tomorrow.

And... Done

~ for Sierra, mom, and dad
Thursday, March 18

The song, "I've had the Time
of My Life," from *Dirty Dancing*,
made me laugh out loud, standing
in line at the CVS. But the wait
was longer than a pop song,
so I stared at knee braces
and blood sugar kits...
till a voice behind
a curtain said
"next..."

*   *   *

I didn't feel it.
So I wondered if
she'd even stuck it,
you know, in my arm.

Just a smallish Band-Aid
with the wisp of a promise
beneath it—not a good time
for doubt, after a year's-worth
of dying for the thing to happen.
And so many did... while waiting.

    *   *   *

Yesterday marked the one-year
anniversary of the initial entry
I made into what I had no idea
would be a poetic documentary.
And, whether or not it is, indeed,
poetic will be up to bored scholars,
with nothing better to do, to decide.
But, it is a documentary, nonetheless,
whether or not it wins the gold sticker.

Back on March 18th of 2020, I quipped
of how I'd felt conflicted about being
told to keep a "calculated distance."
I made a joke about isolation…
as if I were the Br'er Rabbit
begging not to be tossed
into that briar patch.

    *   *   *

It's not funny now.

I want to hug my daughter.
I want to hug my mom and dad…
without worry of becoming their death.

That's why last night, after filming
Take 103 of the Fire Pit Sessions,
I stood in front of the bathroom
mirror to remove the Band-Aid.

I had to see the crimson speck
of proof. I needed to see that
stain on the little white pad.

I needed the blood
of a bit of hope.

FERTILE GROUND

~ for Ôstara, goddess of the spring equinox
Saturday, March 20

The end of winter was once
a more celebrated occasion,
back before electric heaters
and burning of fossil fuels.

Ôstara brings us renewal
and rebirth… sounds like
goddess of resilience to me.
Guiding us through and out
of the long darkness of 2020.

She also gave us Easter, because
the Christians were sick of pagans
bogarting all the fun of the new sun
as it arrives with increasing warmth
here in the season of our friskiness.

We owe her the white bunny as well,
hiding eggs for the kids, who have no
idea it gave birth to odd phrases like
"horny as…" or "going at it like…"

But let's not spoil a beautiful day
with a thing as crass as history.

Let us instead build a flicker fire
beneath the half Worm Moon

and welcome what is now
beginning to stir below…

among the dirt and stones,
as well as in other regions.

If There Ever Was One

~ for Adam Zagajewski
(June 21, 1954 to March 21, 2021)
Monday, March 22

In one of your early poems, you wrote:

> The German on the café terrace
> held a small book on his lap.
> I caught sight of the title:
> *Mysticism for Beginners.*

From that I learned
that as little as 22
skillfully chosen words
can be worth a thousand
pictures. I am still grateful.

I'll never forget how gentle
and quiet your voice was
over pasta and a salad
among the thoughtless
banter in that crowded
café of our own, the one
with televisions in the bar,

nor how true, how genuinely
rapt your smile looked when
my eight-year-old daughter

offered her unique insights
to the heavy conversation.

A number of your books
sit on a shelf about two
feet from my right elbow,
as I write with my left hand
every morning that I am home.
All of them sad there'll be no more
little brothers or sisters come to roost.

You left us on World Poetry Day.
I shook my head... Seriously?

Then, I took my hat off...
held it fast to my chest...
and whispered, *Seriously.*

GRUMPUS

~ for Charles Bukowski
Tuesday, March 23

If UNESCO ever voted
to inaugurate a Poet Laureate
of the Pandemic, I would surely
be the first to heave a waving hand
and nominate you, Charles Bukowski.

Because it was you who taught me how
to sift through the madness and debris
of life's disasters, to thoughtfully look
at each scorched and shattered piece,
and pick out which shards to keep.

You helped me understand that
ones who would risk the health
and lives of others, for nothing
more than a perceived political
right, will always live among us.

Poetic justice is seldom served
to ignorance as blissful as theirs.

You reminded me that even an old
misanthropic grumpus could love
his daughter beyond reason, cry

when a horse is wounded, sing
of a bluebird hiding in his heart.

You slapped me hard on the back
and laughed into the unrelenting
darkness during my worst years,

when most of those around me
were just quoting Romans 8:28
and saying they would pray for
the soul slipping away in me.

You knew where all this
was headed, as well as
where it wasn't. So,

I nominate you…
whether UNESCO
pulls through or not.

Leaving Us Lonesome

~ for Larry McMurtry
Thursday, March 25

When a great author
dies in the night,
like you did,
last night,
there comes
a different kind
of silence, the silence
of a million great words
corralled within the pages
for the ages to reconsider…
and academics to fuss over…
in perpetuity, and to no avail.

I think, though I don't know,
what you cared about more
was the cowboy or maybe
cotton-picker who might
sit beneath a shade tree
to read *Lonesome Dove*
or *Leaving Cheyenne*.

What I appreciate,
as much as your work,
is the license you give me,

as a writer, to be from
the part of this country
I was born and raised in.

Someone had to prove
to the Left and Right
Coasts something
was going on
out here.

If I had
a worn-out
Stetson Roper,
I'd tip it your way.

Though… I doubt
you had one either.

YOUR FAULT

~ for Stephen Dunn
Friday, March 26

I read your poem, back on page 183,
"At the Smithville Methodist Church,"
I don't know, some 30 years ago…
maybe more… and that was it—
the end of ever having a real job.
A beautiful affliction, this thing,
poetry. I don't mean to blame you.
But I suppose I am anyway. You said,
at the end of the third stanza, "cynicism,
that other sadness" and I wanted to know
more. Please go on, I thought. Then, later,
you questioned if you could tell a daughter
"the Bible is a great book certain people
use to make you feel bad?" and I might
have said out loud, in public, Holy shit!
Me too! But at the bottom of the page,
just before I turned it to find yet more
gold, you said, "Soon it became clear
to us: you can't teach disbelief to
a child," and that… yes that
was the breaking point.
I hung my head…
turned to the Fates…
and asked where to sign.

Thank You. And I'm Sorry.

~ for those who read all four of these books
Saturday, March 27

First, thank you.
Second, I'm sorry.

I know I did go on
about certain things,
that inherent danger
in keeping a daily log.
There is a furiousness
that too often forgets.

Yet, in my sad defense,
there was a politicalness
that was equally relentless,
a turd that I never asked for,
as if the coronavirus ever gave
anyone a minute's break either.

So, these pages are chocked full
of repetitions—but only because
masking and quarantine offered
very little in the way of options.

Much like Trump's intellectual
prowess delivered no variety.

237

On the one hand, there was
his evil narcissism, and then,
on the other, narcissistic evil.
So don't shoot the messenger.

What I can claim? and, with no
reservation? I've given this effort
my honest, and my dead-level, best.
How literate my dead-level best was?
the sharks are already circling the boat,
and my hands are dripping with blood
for those who mistakenly believe
that poetry's chief occupation
should be to pet our heads
and whisper, *There there.*

Resilience is work,
not comfort, or
a quick snack.

Resilience is:
a tired young
man carrying
a grandmother
in a wheelbarrow
all the way to some
border of some dream

the two of them still share.
The reason why Americans
worry me, and wear me out.

But I love you, my friends and
fellow Amazon Prime members.

Oh hell… there I go again…
no wonder my wife's dying
for me to take a year off
from writing a poem
every damn day.

And I know,
she's right.

But…

SLÀINTE MHATH

~ for Julie and Farrel Droke, from Anne Harris
Sunday, March 28

Of course science has its formulas.
There are actual Units of Resilience
and Toughness, even a Modulus of
Resilience. But I am talking about
the Solid Material of Friendship:
how much energy some people
are able to absorb or withstand
without snapping or breaking.

Who you call when the night is
dark and the tire is flat. The ones
there at the weddings, and certainly
at the funerals. Just a short drive away,
they're there with the broccoli casserole,
or a cold dark Guinness, when necessary.

These are the ones who bring the stinky
cheese and that sweet wine to the tight-
knit party you hold on Christmas Eve.

The ones who know to sneak a little
of the dough along with the cookies,
because they know it's the best part.

The ones who go with you and believe
as well in the Blessing of the Animals
each year at Saint John's Episcopal.

They're fresh flowers and candles
at Jazz in June... or lawn chairs
set out for the Summer Breeze.

And, they're the foremost reason
we can survive a time like this one.

OTHER SIDE-EFFECTS MAY INCLUDE

~ for Eric Clow
Monday, March 29

Our muscles bore more weight
back in the days of normalcy.

I may have lost the particular
set of them that coordinates
lifting and shoving a suitcase
up and into an overhead bin.

Dad was still golfing last year.
Now just getting the bag-full
of clubs into the rack in back
of the cart would take effort.

You were walking, with help,
when this whole mess began
to close doors, and all they
serve as metaphors for,
firmly in our hopeful
faces.
      Now there's way
too much time in each day
to sit and think way too much
about it and too many other things.

We need those tiny universes that
spiral in every one of our atoms
to find ways to communicate
over these new distances...

through the thick walls
of this stock-stillness,
down the dark halls
of stern isolation,

then back out
those doors.

WHAT POETS DO

~ Beth Wood
Tuesday, March 30

You did the thing…
the thing we all should do,
that so few ever get around to.

You stepped outside your life,
as it was, turned the new self
around to face it, and then

took back that wild ball
of rumpled feathers…
the roughed-up bird…

holding it fast and hard
in a matriarch's embrace
as you hit some sky-road

to a better-next—as only
a real traveler knows how.
Kids, don't try this at home.

You once described my heart
as "that tiny little rusted orb
somebody else threw away"

that my better-next picked up
"for a song" at the junkyard.
I'll never be able to return

a favor, or truth, as simply
correct as that. Thank you.
As another songwriter said,

"Cuz that's what poets do."
Though... I think he meant
something quite else by that.

But let's not dwell. No, instead,
let's raise our glasses and lean over
the mountains between us for a toast.

OUR ANGER

~ for Milton Brasher-Cunningham
Wednesday, March 31

For you, it's a huge dark reservoir
that came to you in a dream lately
(a lake that expands its banks ever
and on) by virtue of nothing more
than remaining alive enough years
to know now that being precious,
true, or good doesn't save a thing.

For David Whyte, a poet we both
revere, it is "the deepest form of
compassion," for all that we love
and hope to protect and care for.

For me, it's the reason I've been
in therapy for longer than some
would care for me to remember,
but also long enough to come to
the conclusion that a cure for it
may not be what I want after all.

Those who might have looked
to me to render them happier
stopped reading these poems
early last summer, or before.

Emerging from the turbid cloud
of Covid-19, whether this year
or next, our anger, channeled
into a constructive presence
and form of action, will play
as much a role as peace, love,
and understanding ever have...
or will.

      Hell, even the son of God
threw the tables of money changers
in the face of a temple's desecration.

April,
and some
of May ... ...

Poetry summons us to life, to courage
in the face of the growing shadow.

~ Adam Zagajewski

GRAND SHROOMPA, POET WARRIOR

~ for Art Goodtimes
Friday, April 2

There's a fine tradition of failed
acolytes and wayward disciples,
young tub-thumping idealogues,
growing up to become more useful
to the truer needs of the people—
possibly even, dare I say, to God?
as long as it turns out our deeper
suspicion (that God is the trees,
the stones, the sun and rain
that cover them) is true,

but also the other
suspicion that
the Vatican II,
and the Southern
Baptist Convention,
are filled with demons
and soiled sold-out angels
in plush robes and dark suits
who harbor fatal Freudian issues
with their mothers that they project
on the Virgen Mary and every other
young and innocent thing in sight.

So of course that one year on the Crow
Reservation followed by the Summer
of Love, back in Haight-Ashbury?
would be the beginning to an end
that, down so many hard roads,
would become a new beginning
that found you up Bear Creek
with, miraculously, a paddle.
The great paddle of poetry.

And so it both was and is
that a good Bontempi boy
became the Goodtimes man,
Grand Master Parade Shroompa
of the Telluride Mushroom Festival,
overseer of the Annual MycoLuscious
MycoLicious MycoLogical Poetry Show,

as well as the cardinal Poet Laureate of
Colorado's Western Slope, for which
we are, and will forever be, grateful.

Anonymous

~ for Patrick Marshall
Saturday, April 3

We see the advantages
every time we turn on the news
or scan the front page of *The Times*.

The headline seldom works out well
for all those involved—especially if
the story continues onto Page 7A.

Poets have to jump off bridges
or stick their heads in ovens
to be interesting enough.

Bukowski says, "I see
Hemingway cleaning
his shotgun," and,
we get what he means.

The lesser-known Zagajewski
describes our monkish occupation:

> waiting motionless,
> flipping pages, patient meditation,
> passivities not pleasing
> to that judge with the greedy gaze.

Until she came down with poetry,
my daughter hated sitting with me
in the corners of old coffee shops.

Sadly for her though, a noticeably
beautiful woman is never allotted
a healthy amount of anonymity.

Yet, her skills with navigating
the profanities of urban society
continue to astonish and awe me.

How do I explain the extent to which
I want to be widely read and fairly well
unknown at the same time? We'd need
a young Einstein to concoct that theory.

It makes me sound like the Unabomber.
Which worries me because of how much
I also want to dwell alone in some cabin
in the woods outside Lincoln, Montana.

But don't worry... I failed mathematics
and couldn't have made it into Harvard.

The First Step

~ for Barbara Blanks
Sunday, April 4

For not yet a year now,
we've been surrounded,
it seems, by more idiots
than ever before; though
it is possible they've been
there all along. It's just that
they have dropped the masks
they once hid behind, and now,
we can see their mouths and noses
for what they are, and what they spew.

So, in order to understand them better,
in the hope of learning to communicate,
since logic is out of the question, I have
decided I should try to get in touch with
the idiot inside of me… get to know its
idiotic ways, and why it's such an idiot.
As I am told is very much the case…
by some friendly idiots around me.

The Hindus might have said,

> *The idiot in me bows*
> *to the idiot in you.*

255

But they didn't.
And the divine is not
what we're discussing here.

What we need is a foundation,
a place to begin.
                    Therefore,
might I suggest we stand
before this large group
assembled here today
and take the first step:

Hi, my name is Nathan,
      and I am an idiot.

THE POINT OF NEIGHBORS

~ for Patrick Marshall
Monday, April 5

This year has reminded me, or
maybe taught me to begin with,
that a little boy trying to put air
in his bicycle tires in Tataouine,
Tunisia is as much my neighbor
as the Booths across the street.

8 billion people and counting
does not allow for those old
distances we killed to keep.

I can hop on a pressurized
can of beans and be there
to help him with his bike
in less than a long day.

100 years ago, it would
have taken me a month.

It's not that the big dream
of nationalism is politically
naïve and flies in the face
of every parable Jesus
and Mister Rogers

strove to instill in us.
It is more so, and simply,
that the dream is empirically
useless, and logistically futile.

We are now at what I will call
the Neighboring Point, a new
scientific theory that means,
in layman's terms: We will
do this thing together,

or this damn thing
will not get done.

A FRIEND ONCE

~ for Sergio Gypsy
Tuesday, April 6

You were the most beautifully mad
and deftly insane dear old friend
I ever hated to have to let go—
sort of a godfather I referred to
as *uncle*, though you were neither.

We once had what you once called
"a twice parapseudical psychological
metamusical thing" going for us—
we could write 5 to 10 songs a day.

But as you also said, *That was then.*
But, this is not then now... a thing
I suspect someone said already.
Though, I never found it out.

To say "I miss you" is both
true, and, not necessarily so.
We were a bit much overall,
when we worked in tandem.

So for its own good sake,
the world likely needs us
the way that we are now.

WHAT I WILL AND WON'T

~ for Anne Roberts
Wednesday, April 7

What I Won't Go Back To

… is one inch less
   than a six-foot clearance
   from people I do not know

… are the friends I opened up and
   found black mold in their closet

… is the killing field of a deranged
   pseudo-Christian cult populated
   by folks I once thought to know
   better, who appear to think Jesus
   was a machinegun-toting capitalist
   with sallow skin and a casino empire

… is the big illusion that cars and highways,
   planes and their skyways, or trains rattling
   down their tracks will ever someday sate
   my ragamuffin-gadabout-vagabond soul

What I Will Go Back To

… is the bar at Maria's

… is closing the distance between
my parents, and my daughter

… are the few friends I found
I can argue Hemingway with,
pour more wine, and move on,
who take me as I am—a rather
passionate, and a fairly fiendish,
poet nutjob who gets a little more
of each quality as he sips on tequila

… are the cathedrals of the mountains,
the temples of the seas… the altars
of stones… the liturgy of trees…
the prayers of the flowers…
the Theology of Dirt

… are the roads that matter,
the planes—if I must—that
carry me to you, and the trains,
as long as each car is a poem
delivering a dream of hope

Where It All Ends

~ for Jan Ohmstede
Thursday, April 8

I gave it my best
to respond every day
to this Willy-Wonka year,
among the strangest in history.

I have handled politics and religion
with the same studied consideration,
and utter contempt, when deserved,
which was clearly most of the time.

And, before the first poem in
the first book of this series,
I quoted my favorite poet
to try and cover my ass:

> To register what it feels like to be
> alive in a particular moment in
> history is an enormous task.
> ~ Stephen Dunn

So it is that each piece should
have been burned at the stake
of all those evenings I've spent
reading them over in the fire pit,

incendiary soldiers that they were,
just following the orders I'd given,
returning to ash and dust, as will we.
As will this, and every other, book...

whether by the hand of the next Hitler,
or the Earth, in her own flames of time.
And to her I will say, Just remember...
I busted my fingers, elbows, and back

building that monument in your honor.
So remember too, when the time comes
I have to leave it, it will burn, burn, burn.
It will singe, and sear, the skin of my soul.

VIS-À-VIS

~ for Danna Primm
Friday, April 9

For eleven-ish months
and three-ish days now
I have been performing
before a physical audience
of limestones and cedar trees,
while smiling into a camera lens
barely more than a millimeter wide.

I mentioned this in a previous poem,
but months have passed since then.

And so, to the virtual audience…
no… wait… the very real folks
who have tuned in virtually…

(forgive me, but a lot of lines
have been blurred these days).

Anyway, to those who watched,
my gratitude is as deep as you are
real, not virtual. And though I love,
worship even, the stones and trees,
I long for the day when I will see
someone's eyes roll after I say

something stupid in a show,
or look at the watch when
I go a few minutes over.

I cannot wait to make
mistakes and blunders
that cannot be deleted.

Yes, bring on the days
when we gather again
face to face to face,
soul to heart to
heart to soul.

The Fundamental Things Apply

~ for Karen Zundel
Saturday, April 10

A breeze, lazing through
the library's open window,
has flipped five or so pages
of the calendar into some
future month. One more
little draft, and it will be
October, or November.

And it's hard to imagine
the year that's coming
when it will be hard
to imagine the year
that's just passed.

A bizarre epoch
that our kids will
someday remove
their huge bifocals
and squint to recall
in deteriorating detail
to our great-grandkids.

"Oh, dear God… 2020…"

I just looked at a photograph
of my wife and I, from the time
we met, about fourteen years ago,
and it's not fair that only one of us
appears to be aging. You can guess
which one it would most likely be.

Apparently the decades have
marched a fair bit harder
through the streets
of my worn face.

And so it goes
that the headline:

Year of the Pandemic

will eventually gather dust,
much like the yellowing
pages of this book.

BEARING WITNESS

~ for Molly Griffis, from Anne Harris
Sunday, April 11

The great tellers of stories
are the ones who learned
early on to listen to them,

like a doe above her fawn
harkening for the footfalls
of a scrawny mountain lion.

There's always a storyteller
lurking in the faraway past
of a teller telling one now.

Yet, the better among us
are the fierce preservers,
the guardians of all story.

*   *   *

Champion of libraries, books,
the authors and the illustrators,
you were the one who gave life

to the little bookstore that could,
Levite of Apache—a magic den
of unraked leaves of literature,

Pendleton blankets, the art
of those who bedeck words
with pictures—and all of this

within walking distance of my
house. After his passing, you
gave me your husband's works

of Arthur Conan Doyle, his copy
of *The Private Life of Sherlock Holmes*,
clothbound, bearing the bookplate

EX LIBRIS — Griffis — along
with a bronze bust of Mark Twain
that sits defiantly among my stones.

You've been a witness to the great
storytellers. You are also a witness
to our lives. And so, please know

that we will now take our turn,
from here and ever onward,
bearing witness to yours.

TIME NOW

~ for Kathryn McGregor
Tuesday, April 13

She wished for a mask
that covered her eyes
as well. I've imagined
one that plugs my ears.

The news is too thrilled
with the science of death,
    the latest way to do it…
    ghost bodies in ICUs…

the shouts of protestors,
volleying back and forth
street-side to street-side,
who cannot all be right.

But another gun goes
off, in Minneapolis…
and the echo ricochets
louder, then louder still.

And flash-bang grenades
tattoo our tired retinas…
while the ongoing sighs
of nurses can't drown

the cries of the patients.
And, we had longed for
some kind of end to it...
but she and I both know

it's time to train our eyes
and ears on better signs
and sounds—the dimly
glowing horizon ahead,

those lightning strikes
of newfound dreams,
the thunder of hope
up in the distance.

Sheesh…

Whatever they suggested
the side-effects might be…
for a second Moderna dose…
they were right to suggest them.

By 2:35 a.m., I was figuring out
that I would not escape the year
without a good shoulder-shake
and body-rock to the joints,
but especially lower back.

At 4:47, I was sipping
on my water like that
slumped over cowboy
in the dusty high plains
of some Clint Eastwood
movie I can't quite recall?
The one when he throws his
bone-dry canteen in the sand?
Though, that might have been
a different western altogether.

Anyway, by 5:53-something,
I considered going in to grab
that half of a margarita I put

in the freezer last night, because
I did not want to risk a headache.
Why not go out with a good buzz.

Then, when I finally had to give up,
I was barely able to stand. I paused
for a bit… covered all my options.

But when I attempted to put on
my pajama pants, I could not
get my second foot to go in.

So, I had to shuffle over to
an ottoman and sit for a while,
think about what I wanted to be,
you know, when I grow up someday.

NOT TODAY

I will do nothing today.
In Western Civilization terms:
I will not accomplish anything today.
My apologies to Manifest Destiny, and
this great country—with its collective
case of Restless Leg Syndrome. But,
my bones will not play your game.
Even things I have no choice on,
like getting to the bathroom,
require a bit of planning.

And it's a darn good thing
oatmeal knows how to cook
itself in a about a cup of water.
Otherwise I would not be eating.

If I can muster up anything at all...
I might stare out the window a while.
I might even consider the third episode
of that Ken Burns documentary on Papa
Hemingway, just so I can feel better
about myself as an author who is
trying to remain a human too.
But that's as crazy as I'll get.

IT APPEARS

~ for Alexis Rowe
Sunday, April 18

When an angel appears,
the world changes, again.

As the world seems always
in some need of change…

that's why the angels sing
their poems and stories…

they've learned what it takes
to make a world stop and listen.

THE MUSES

~ for Alexis Rowe
Monday, April 19

When nine fiery sisters
go into business together…

daughters of the God of Thunder
and the Goddess of Remembrance…

what chance does any poor soul have
against their powers of inspiration,

when it comes to the dreamers
who wield paper and a pen.

THE CONVICTED

~ for Derek Chauvin
Tuesday, April 20

It does no good for me
to fist bump the empty air
around my TV, to watch your
eyes flit back and forth… afraid
to land on some jury member,
or a closed-circuit camera…
as Judge Cahill reads it out…
"Guilty… Guilty… Guilty…"
as I wonder if hearing that said
three times helps it to sink in…
past the mind blocks you've built.

The last time I wrote to you, I made
mention of your 'now mostly over life.'
Does it do any better for me to suggest
that it doesn't have to be? Not totally?
Even where you'll spend it, there is
one last freedom that you could
avail yourself of if you decide
to do more with your time
than eat and shit, and die.

You could also… change.

A WAY OF THINGS

There are worse
things I suppose,

than a good thing,
born of a bad thing,

coming to a good end,
even if the end feels bad.

So, here I am at the good
end of a good thing. And,

it feels more sad than bad.
A good sad I'd have to say.

The kind of good sad ending
that, so often, seems to lead to
some kind of good new beginning.

BLUE ROCK

~ for Billy & Dodee Crockett
Tuesday, May 18

In the beginning
was a picnic table
sitting in the shade
among not quite a
formless void, but
more a cedar grove.

Then came a dream
that was followed by
a mountain of blueish
stones, and a master
of the mason's craft.

After the years it took
for the final rock to be
placed... I read a poem
in the soft, yellowy light
of a new and great room.

So began a generation of songs,
performances, melody, and magic,
late-night laughter and tears around
a fire's glow, and all beneath a tower
made of sunsets and red wine toasts.

I lost a game of Scrabble to Ellis
Paul up in the top of that tower
when he whipped out a bogus
nautical term no one had ever
heard of. Not in this century.

But, I also finished a long
and tortuous dissertation
at the oak desk that sits
looking out the window,
there, in the Olive Room,
one cold December in 2004.

A couple of years later, I met
Jimmy LaFave, the man who
would later introduce me to
my wife, who has walked
with me into the better
parts of a recovered life.

My daughter smiled here,
was inspired here, during
a dark, undeserved decade.

I recorded albums here—albums
that make me sound better than I am.

And while the stories, memories,
and gifts by no means end there,
this will have to stop somewhere.

I am afraid that I passed the exit
for good poetry a few miles back.

But still, a benediction is in order…
a skill I should've learned from my father.

And since I did not, I'm reduced to this:

However a dictionary defines 'friend,'
you two have been more than
whatever that is to me.

And so, this is
my meager
thanks.

CHRIST AGAIN

~ for David Slemmons
Monday, May 24

I know a poet
who has to have
his voice removed
because of cancer...

having grabbed him
by the throat... again.

He's been Christ more
than once... I'm afraid.

And there's no such thing
as 'the final insult'... not
when it comes to poets
and accidental prophets.

But... this is a big one.

And I will slap the first
person who says "irony"
out loud. Not out of spite,
but out of duty, and honor,
to our weird unspoken code.

Sometimes continuing to breathe
is a protest against the vagaries.

It is a fight to the death, when
death is taking his damn time
to do us in. Cheeky bastard.

Meanwhile, the surgeon gets
richer, an insurance company
a penny poorer,
                    and the poet
has to learn to speak in some
new way,
              because that's
what poets do.

OUR BEARINGS

~ for those who are ready
Sunday, May 30

It was the first time
I'd performed in front
of human faces, live, in,
let me count, 15 months.

Many of them, smiling…
most of them with hands
clapping just below them,
as I recounted a wild year.

I felt a bit of a warm-fuzzing,
a spirit-buzzing, as one by one
I remembered things, like where
the guitar goes, how to use a capo,

but, mainly, how hard it is for me to
keep my head up and my eyes open
when I sing… I never bothered
for the walls and the iPhone.

My voice cracked, I dropped
lines, I had to cut some songs
and a few poems from the set
I'd carefully planned and timed,

because, poets are worse than
preachers, when it comes to
abusing their allotment—
as if you didn't know.

But the walls echoed
with laughter, hearts
tendered forgiveness
to the prodigal bard…

and eyes belied a hunger,
as if gathering around a fire
for a good story was the thing
we've been living and dying for,

for the last… long year…
if not 10,000 of them.

Numbering the Days

~ for Doug Hanks
and one from June

Of all the stories to come my way
along the path of this bizarre,
otherworldly year, yours
is certainly the story
to end this one.

147 days.
46 of those
on a ventilator,
unconscious, out…
unaware of a thousand
prayers on the tips of a thousand
tongues, keeping their whispered vigils…

147 days of scrubs, stethoscopes, tubes,
and heads shaking over your chart…

days of EMTs, drivers, firefighters,
but especially Captain Rich Toll…
the first one through the door…

days of doctors predicting your
likely loss of the wicked game.

And for 78 much longer days,
you did not see, nor touch,
your wife... a wife who
stayed close in spirit...

the wife who brought
your reborn body and
reviving soul back home
to the curbside celebration
on Sapphire Street... of signs
waving... dear friends cheering.

And, though it will take 365 or more
days to recover, you will take each one
by the hand, and the grace of God...
with grapefruit and coffee, flowers
and guitars...
                    turning graves
into gardens... sorrow
into salvation.

Also by Nathan Brown

Author Bio

Nathan Brown is an author, songwriter, and award-winning poet living in Wimberley, Texas. He holds a PhD in English and Journalism from the University of Oklahoma and taught there for over twenty years. He also served as Poet Laureate for the State of Oklahoma in 2013 and 2014.

He's published over 20 books. Among them is *100 Years, To Sing Hallucinated: First Thoughts on Last Words,* and *Just Another Honeymoon in France: A Vagabond at Large,* a travel memoir that marks the first in a coming series.

His anthology *Oklahoma Poems, and Their Poets* was a finalist for the Oklahoma Book Award. *Karma Crisis: New and Selected Poems* was a finalist for the Paterson Poetry Prize. And his earlier book, *Two Tables Over,* won the 2009 Oklahoma Book Award.

For more, go to: **brownlines.com**

MEZCALITA
PRESS

An independent publishing company
dedicated to bringing the printed poetry,
fiction, and non-fiction of musicians who
want to add to the power and reach
of their important voices.

For more, go to: **mezpress.com**

CPSIA information can be obtained
at www.ICGtesting.com
Printed in the USA
LVHW111636080721
692036LV00001BA/9

9 781734 869248